Luan Ferr

Shamanic Healing
The Power of Ancient Traditions

Original Title: Cura Xamânica - O Poder Curativo das Antigas Tradições
Copyright © 2024 by Luiz Antonio dos Santos
Second Edition
This is the second edition of Shamanic Healing, revised and expanded to offer readers a richer and more detailed experience of ancestral shamanic practices and their contemporary applications.

This book explores shamanism and its ancestral practices tailored to contemporary needs, integrating physical, emotional, and spiritual dimensions for healing and self-awareness. It is intended for reflection, study, and personal growth and does not replace professional medical or psychological guidance.

Production Team for the Second Edition
Author: Luan Ferr
Revision: Helena Ribeiro
Adaptation and Collaboration: Virginia Moreira dos Santos
Translation: Michael Carter
Graphic Design and Layout: Arthur Mendes da Costa
Cover: Anderson Casagrande Neto

Publication and Identification
Shamanic Healing / By Luan Ferr
Booklas.com, 2024
Categories: Body, Mind, and Spirit. Spirituality.
DDC: 158.1 - CDU: 613.8

All Rights Reserved
Publisher: Booklas / Luiz Antonio dos Santos
Rua José Delalíbera, 962
86.183-550 – Cambé – PR – Brazil
Email: suporte@booklas.com
Website: www.booklas.com

Contents

Foreword 4
Chapter 1 Anxiety and Stress 15
Chapter 2 Insomnia 26
Chapter 3 Depression 38
Chapter 4 Emotional Blocks 51
Chapter 5 Chronic Fatigue 65
Chapter 6 Chronic Pain 76
Chapter 7 Digestive Problems 87
Chapter 8 Respiratory Problems 99
Chapter 9 Circulatory Problems 110
Chapter 10 Skin Problems 121
Chapter 11 Immunity problems 131
Chapter 12 Self-esteem Problems 141
Chapter 13 Fears and Phobias 152
Chapter 14 Relationship Problems 162
Chapter 15 Sadness and Grief 172
Chapter 16 Lack of Purpose 181
Chapter 17 Financial Problems 192
Chapter 18 Addictions and Dependencies 202
Chapter 19 Spiritual Problems 212
Chapter 20 Energy Problems 224
Epilogue 234
Bibliographic References 236

Foreword

Shamanism is an ancient spiritual practice that originated thousands of years ago, transcending cultural and geographical boundaries. It is found in various forms in indigenous cultures around the world, including Native Americans, Siberian peoples and Australian Aborigines. Shamanic practice is centered on the belief that everything in the universe is interconnected and that shamans, as intermediaries between the physical and spiritual worlds, possess the power to access these realms to heal and guide their communities.

Shamans are known for their ability to enter altered states of consciousness, usually induced by practices such as meditation, rhythmic dance, the use of entheogenic plants or the constant beating of drums. These states allow shamans to communicate with nature spirits, ancestors and other spiritual beings. This communication is used to gain knowledge, diagnose illnesses and perform cures, as well as protecting and guiding the community.

The role of the shaman varies according to the culture, but generally includes the functions of healer, spiritual advisor and ceremonial leader. Shamans are respected for their wisdom and skills and are often seen as guardians of ancestral knowledge and spiritual traditions. Shamanic practice emphasizes the importance of harmony between human beings and nature, recognizing that individual well-being is intrinsically linked to the balance of the natural world.

At the heart of shamanism is the idea that everything has a spirit, be it a stone, a tree, an animal or a human being. This animist perspective sees the world as a vibrant fabric of interconnected energy, where each element has life and purpose. The shaman is able to connect with these spirits to gain wisdom and guidance, helping to restore balance when it is disturbed.

Shamanic rituals are varied and can include purification ceremonies, such as the use of sacred herbs for smoking, the construction of sand or stone mandalas, and the creation of altars dedicated to the guardian spirits. These practices are carried out with the intention of curing illnesses, resolving conflicts and bringing spiritual clarity. The preparation for these rituals is meticulous, requiring the shaman and the participants to be in a state of purity and concentration.

Shamanic healing is not limited to the physical aspect, but also encompasses the mental, emotional and spiritual levels. The shaman understands that many illnesses have their roots in spiritual imbalances or emotional traumas, and that true healing requires a holistic approach that integrates all aspects of the being. Through healing rituals, the shaman works to remove energy blockages, restore the flow of vital energy and reintegrate the person into their own spiritual power.

In addition to healing practices, shamans also play a crucial role in spiritual guidance. They help people understand their life journeys, offering advice and rituals to overcome challenges and find their way back to balance. Shamanic wisdom is passed down from generation to generation, keeping alive the connection with ancestors and the continuity of spiritual traditions.

The benefits of shamanism are vast and encompass physical, mental and spiritual healing. Shamanic practices offer tools to deal with stress and anxiety, promote self-discovery and strengthen the connection with nature. By accessing heightened states of consciousness, people can find creative solutions to problems, experience a deep sense of peace and harmony, and develop a richer and more meaningful understanding of life.

For those wishing to embark on a shamanic journey, it is essential to start with an open mind and a receptive heart. The practice of shamanism requires dedication, respect and a genuine desire to learn and grow. When preparing for this journey, it is important to set clear intentions and connect with your own spirituality, always seeking guidance from the spirits and ancestral wisdom.

This is the beginning of a transformative journey, where shamanism offers a path to healing, wisdom and reconnection with the spiritual and natural world.

The practice of shamanism involves deep interaction with nature and its elements. Earth, air, water and fire are seen as living forces, each with its own energy and spirit. Shamans use these forces in their rituals to bring healing and balance. Earth represents stability and nourishment, air symbolizes thought and communication, water is linked to emotions and intuition, and fire represents transformation and vital energy.

Nature spirits, such as the spirits of plants, animals and minerals, play a vital role in shamanic practice. Each spirit possesses specific wisdom and power, and the shaman can call on them for assistance in healings and other ceremonies. For example, certain animals are considered spirit guides and can offer protection, insight and strength. Medicinal plants are used both physically and spiritually to treat illness and promote well-being.

To connect with these spirits, the shaman often uses techniques such as the shamanic journey. During the journey, the shaman enters an altered state of consciousness and travels to the spirit world in search of wisdom and healing. This state can be achieved through meditation, the repetition of mantras or the rhythmic beating of drums. The shamanic journey allows the shaman to explore different spiritual realms, meet spirit guides and gain insights into the patient's condition.

Shamanic instruments, such as drums, rattles and healing sticks, are essential tools in the shaman's work. These instruments are used to alter states of consciousness, invoke spirits and channel healing energy. The drum, in particular, is a powerful instrument whose rhythmic beats help the shaman enter trance states and connect with the spirit world. Each instrument is considered sacred and is treated with great respect.

Preparation for shamanic rituals is a crucial aspect of the practice. Before performing a ritual, the shaman goes through a purification process that can include fasting, herbal baths and meditation. The intention is to cleanse the body and mind of any impurities and focus on the spiritual task ahead. Participants in the rituals are also encouraged to purify themselves and prepare their minds and hearts for the experience.

Shamanic rituals take place in places considered sacred, such as forests, mountains, rivers and caves. These places are chosen for their special energy and the presence of guardian spirits. The nature of these places helps to amplify the power of the ritual and facilitate the connection with the spiritual realms. In addition, the timing of the ritual can be influenced by natural cycles, such as the phases of the moon, the seasons and other astrological phenomena.

During a ritual, the shaman can use chants, dances and other forms of artistic expression to invoke spirits and channel healing energy. Chants are usually passed down from generation to generation and are considered sacred. They are used to establish a connection with the spirits, invoke their presence and ask for their help. Shamanic dance is another important practice that helps to move energy and enter a trance state.

Shamanic healing is a profound process that goes beyond treating physical symptoms. The shaman works to identify and treat the root cause of the problem, which is often related to spiritual imbalances or emotional trauma. The aim is to restore harmony and balance, not only in the individual, but also in the community and the natural world. Healing can involve removing negative energies, recovering lost parts of the soul and restoring the flow of vital energy.

At the end of the rituals, there is often a period of integration, where the shaman and the participants reflect on the experience and share their insights. This moment is crucial for assimilating the changes and healings that have taken place, and for understanding how to apply these lessons in daily life. Integration is seen as an essential part of the healing process, helping to solidify the spiritual transformations and ensure that the benefits of the ritual are long-lasting.

This dive into shamanic practices and beliefs reveals the depth and richness of this spiritual tradition. Shamanism offers a powerful path to healing, connection with the sacred and harmonization with the universe, inviting everyone to explore and discover their own spiritual journeys.

Shamanism is a practice that emphasizes healing and personal transformation through connection with the spirit world and nature. This holistic practice sees the human being as an integral part of the universe, where everything is interconnected and has a vital energy. The central belief of shamanism is that many illnesses and problems are caused by imbalances or blockages of this vital energy, and that healing can be achieved by restoring the balance and flow of energy.

Shamans play a crucial role as healers, not only treating physical symptoms, but also addressing the emotional, mental and spiritual aspects of illness. The holistic view of shamanism recognizes that health depends on harmony between body, mind and spirit, and that true healing involves reintegrating these parts into a cohesive whole.

One of the fundamental tools of shamanism is the purification ceremony. These ceremonies can include smoking with sacred herbs, such as sage, cedar or fennel, which are burned to cleanse negative energies and purify the environment. The smoke from these herbs is considered an offering to the spirits, helping to establish a connection between the physical and spiritual worlds. Smoking is often used at the beginning of a ritual to prepare the space and the participants for the spiritual work.

Another important aspect of shamanism is the spiritual journey, where the shaman travels to the spiritual realms in search of healing and guidance. These journeys can be carried out in various ways, including deep meditation, the use of drums or other rhythmic instruments, and the ingestion of entheogenic plants in ceremonial contexts. The aim of these journeys is to contact spirit guides, power animals and other spiritual beings who can offer wisdom and assistance.

Shamans also use the energy of natural elements in their rituals. For example, water can be used to cleanse and purify, fire to transform and transmute energies, earth to provide stability and nourishment, and air to bring clarity and communication. These elements are seen as manifestations of the spiritual forces of the universe and are integrated into rituals to amplify the power of healing.

The practice of shamanism requires a deep respect and reverence for nature and the spirits. Shamans often perform offerings and gratitude ceremonies to honor the spirits and ask for their assistance. These offerings can include food, flowers, crystals or other symbolic items that represent an exchange of energy and an acknowledgement of the spiritual support received.

Shamanic healing often involves identifying and removing energy blockages. These blockages can be caused by emotional trauma, negative thoughts or external influences. The shaman works to detect these obstructions and restore the flow of vital energy through various techniques, such as the laying on of hands, the use of healing crystals and the channeling of spiritual energy. Removing these blockages allows vital energy to flow freely, promoting health and well-being.

As well as treating illness, shamanism also focuses on preventing and maintaining health. Shamans teach practices and rituals that can be incorporated into daily life to maintain balance and harmony. These practices can include meditation, breathing techniques, gratitude rituals and regular connection with nature. By integrating these practices, individuals can strengthen their spiritual connection and prevent imbalances before they manifest as illnesses.

The journey of shamanism is one of self-discovery and spiritual growth. Through shamanic practice, people can discover hidden aspects of themselves, overcome fears and limitations, and develop greater understanding and compassion. The personal transformation that occurs through shamanism is profound and lasting, providing a path to spiritual fulfillment and inner harmony.

When exploring shamanism, it is essential to approach this practice with an open mind and a receptive heart. The shamanic journey is unique to each individual, and each person's experience will be shaped by their own intention and willingness to connect with the spiritual. When embarking on this journey, people are invited to trust the process and allow ancestral wisdom and guiding spirits to guide their path to healing and transformation.

Shamanism is not only a healing practice, but also a spiritual path that offers a profound understanding of life and the universe. One of the fundamental beliefs of shamanism is the interconnectedness of all things. This holistic worldview recognizes that every being, whether human, animal, plant or mineral, has a spirit and is connected to the great fabric of life. This interconnectedness implies that the well-being of one affects the well-being of all, and that harmony must be maintained if balance is to be preserved.

Preparation for the shamanic journey is an essential aspect that cannot be underestimated. Before starting a ritual or ceremony, it is important for the shaman and the participants to purify their bodies and minds. This purification process can include fasting, herbal baths and meditation. The aim is to cleanse any negativity or distractions that might interfere with the connection with the spirit world. Careful preparation creates a state of receptivity and openness, allowing the shaman to enter higher states of consciousness more easily.

Spirit guides play a vital role in shamanic practice. They are seen as allies and teachers who help the shaman navigate the spiritual realms and gain valuable insights. Spirit guides can manifest in various forms, including animals, ancestors and divine entities. Each guide has their own wisdom and can offer specific guidance for different situations. The relationship between the shaman and their spirit guides is built up over time and is based on trust and mutual respect.

Communication with the spirits is facilitated by various methods, one of the most common being the shamanic journey. During this journey, the shaman can use the rhythmic sound of a drum or rattle to induce an altered state of consciousness. This state allows the shaman to travel to the spirit world and interact directly with spirit guides. The journey can be undertaken for a specific purpose, such as seeking healing for a patient, obtaining answers to a question or simply deepening the spiritual connection.

The elements of nature are constantly integrated into shamanic practices. Earth, air, water and fire are considered not only as physical components of the world, but as manifestations of spiritual forces. Each element has unique characteristics and can be invoked during rituals to bring balance and healing. For example, earth can be used to provide stability and support, while water can be invoked to cleanse and purify. Invoking these elements helps to harmonize the energy of the ritual and amplify its effects.

Shamanic rituals are performed with great reverence and respect for nature and the spirits. Before starting a ritual, the shaman can make offerings to the spirits to honor them and ask for their assistance. These offerings can include food, flowers, crystals and other symbolic items. The intention behind the offerings is to show gratitude and create an exchange of energy, strengthening the connection between the shaman and the spirit world.

Healing in shamanism is seen as an integral process involving all aspects of the being. Shamans believe that many illnesses have their roots in spiritual imbalances or emotional trauma and that true healing can only be achieved by addressing these underlying causes. Through healing rituals, the shaman works to restore the individual's energetic balance, removing blockages and promoting the free flow of vital energy. This process can include techniques such as the extraction of negative energies, soul retrieval and the channeling of healing energy.

The daily practice of shamanism also includes maintaining balance and harmony through simple rituals and spiritual practices. These can involve morning meditations, gratitude rituals, and practicing mindfulness in nature. Integrating these practices into daily life helps to strengthen the spiritual connection and maintain energetic balance. By living in harmony with shamanic principles, individuals can experience a greater sense of peace, purpose and connection with the universe.

When embarking on the journey of shamanism, it is important to remember that each experience is unique and personal. The path of the shaman is a continuous journey of learning and spiritual growth. Those who dedicate themselves to this practice are invited to explore, experiment and discover their own spiritual truths. Shamanism offers a rich tapestry of wisdom and practices that can enrich anyone's life, providing tools for healing, transformation and connection with the sacred.

The shamanic journey is a deeply transformative experience that allows access to spiritual dimensions and ancestral wisdom. This practice is more than a healing method; it is a spiritual path that leads to self-knowledge and a deeper understanding of the nature of existence. For those who dedicate themselves to shamanism, each ritual and ceremony is an opportunity to grow spiritually and strengthen the connection with the universe.

The importance of intention in shamanism cannot be underestimated. Intention is at the heart of any shamanic spiritual practice. Before starting a ritual, the shaman and the participants set a clear intention, which serves as a guide for the spiritual journey. The intention can be to cure an illness, get answers to an important question or simply seek peace and harmony. A well-defined intention helps to focus energy and direct spiritual efforts effectively.

Connecting with the ancestors is another fundamental aspect of shamanism. Shamans believe that the ancestors, those who lived before us, continue to play an active role in our lives. They are seen as guardians and sources of wisdom, offering guidance and support through the generations. Communication with the ancestors is a vital part of shamanic rituals, and offerings and ceremonies in their honor are performed to keep this connection alive.

Shamanic practice involves a variety of techniques and tools, each with its own purpose and meaning. For example, the technique of soul retrieval is used to recover parts of the soul that may have been lost due to trauma or negative experiences. The shaman enters a trance state and travels to the spirit world to find and reintegrate these lost parts, restoring the individual's fullness and vitality.

Another example is the extraction of negative energies, a technique used to remove harmful influences that may be causing illness or imbalance. The shaman identifies and extracts these energies, using tools such as healing crystals, feathers or other sacred objects. This practice is followed by purification and protection rituals to ensure that the negative energies do not return.

Preparing the sacred space is a crucial step in any shamanic ritual. The space where the ritual will take place is purified and consecrated, creating a safe and sacred environment where spiritual energies can be invoked and directed. This can involve creating a sacred circle, using symbols and invoking the four elements and guardian spirits. A well-prepared space amplifies the effectiveness of the ritual and provides an atmosphere of reverence and respect.

The shaman's role as healer and spiritual guide is multifaceted. As well as performing cures and conducting rituals, the shaman offers ongoing spiritual guidance and support to the community. They help people interpret dreams, understand spiritual messages and make important decisions based on ancestral wisdom. The shaman is a trusted advisor who offers profound insights and practical solutions to life's challenges.

The practice of shamanism also promotes the importance of reciprocity and gratitude. Shamans teach that everything in the universe is interconnected and that the energy we give returns to us. It is therefore essential to practice gratitude and make regular offerings to nature and the spirits. Reciprocity maintains balance and strengthens the relationship with the spirit world, promoting a harmonious and abundant life.

Shamanism offers a unique perspective on life and healing, emphasizing the importance of living in harmony with nature and honoring the spiritual connection with all beings. It is a practice that can transform the way we see the world and relate to it, providing tools for healing, personal transformation and spiritual growth.

At the conclusion of this introduction to shamanism, it is clear that this practice is a profound and enriching path for those seeking a broader understanding of life and the universe. Shamanism invites us to explore our own spiritual journeys, to discover ancient wisdom and to live in harmony with the world around us. With dedication and sincere intention, anyone can embark on this journey and experience the profound transformation that shamanism can bring.

Chapter 1
Anxiety and Stress

Anxiety and stress are common problems that affect many people at various stages of life. These emotional states can manifest in various ways, from constant worry to intense panic attacks. Understanding the nature of these problems is the first step towards addressing them effectively through shamanic practices.

Anxiety is characterized by feelings of apprehension, fear or worry, which can be continuous or arise in response to specific situations. These feelings are often accompanied by physical symptoms, such as palpitations, sweating, tremors and muscle tension. Anxiety can interfere with a person's ability to lead a normal life, affecting their performance at work, their relationships and their general health.

Stress, on the other hand, is the body's response to demands or pressures. While a certain amount of stress can be beneficial, helping to motivate and energize, chronic stress can have harmful effects. Prolonged stress can lead to health problems such as hypertension, heart problems, sleep disorders and digestive problems. In addition, it can aggravate anxiety, creating a vicious cycle that is difficult to break.

The causes of anxiety and stress are varied and can include environmental factors, such as excessive work, family responsibilities and social pressures. Personal factors such as past traumas, genetic predisposition, and mental health problems also play a significant role. Identifying the underlying causes is essential to addressing these problems holistically.

Shamanic healing offers various approaches to treating anxiety and stress, integrating methods that balance the body, mind and spirit. A fundamental practice is the shamanic journey, where the shaman enters an altered state of consciousness to connect with guide spirits and gain insights into the causes and solutions to the problem.

Preparing for a healing ritual for anxiety and stress begins with creating a sacred space. This space should be quiet and free of distractions, allowing for a deep connection with the spiritual world. Purification of the space can be done by burning sacred herbs, such as sage or palo santo, to cleanse any negative energy. The clear intention of healing anxiety and stress should be established, creating a strong foundation for the ritual.

The materials needed for the ritual can include drums or rattles to facilitate entering trance states, healing crystals such as amethyst and rose quartz to promote calm and peace, and essential oils of lavender or chamomile to induce relaxation. The shaman can also prepare an altar with symbols representing the elements of nature, such as shells, stones and feathers, to invoke the presence of the guardian spirits.

The ritual begins with a guided meditation, where the shaman takes the participant into a state of deep relaxation. Rhythmic, controlled breathing is fundamental, helping to calm the mind and prepare the body for the spiritual journey. With the rhythmic sound of the drum, the shaman leads the participant through a visualization, where they meet their spirit guides in a safe and sacred place. These spirits can offer messages of comfort and guidance, helping to relieve anxiety and identify sources of stress.

A crucial part of the ritual is the invocation of healing energy. The shaman channels this energy through their hands or through sacred objects, directing it to areas of the body where tension and stress are most evident. This can be complemented with chants and mantras that reinforce the healing intention and promote a state of inner peace.

At the end of the ritual, it is important to have a period of integration, where the participant reflects on the experience and writes down any insights or messages received. This time of reflection helps to assimilate the healing and bring the necessary changes into daily life. Regular practice of relaxation techniques and maintaining a sacred space in the home can support the continued beneficial effects of the ritual.

Shamanic healing for anxiety and stress is a powerful practice that combines ancient wisdom with modern relaxation techniques. By approaching these problems holistically, it is possible to find a path to inner peace and balance, living a more harmonious and fulfilling life.

Identifying the underlying causes of anxiety and stress is a fundamental step in the shamanic healing process. Often, these conditions are the result of a combination of factors, including traumatic experiences, daily challenges and spiritual imbalances. The shaman works to unravel these factors and understand how they manifest in the individual's body and mind.

Past traumas are often a significant cause of anxiety and stress. Painful or disturbing experiences can leave deep scars, both emotionally and spiritually. These traumas can manifest as irrational fears, recurring nightmares or a constant sense of threat. The shaman uses the spiritual journey to explore these traumas, searching for the source of the suffering and working to release the negative energy associated with these experiences.

Daily challenges and responsibilities also contribute to the accumulation of stress. Situations such as excessive demands at work, financial difficulties or family conflicts can create constant pressure that affects mental and emotional health. The shaman helps to identify these sources of stress and develop strategies to deal with them more effectively, promoting a balanced approach to life.

Spiritual imbalances, although less obvious, are equally important. A disconnection with one's purpose or a lack of alignment with spiritual values can cause a feeling of emptiness and restlessness. The shaman works to restore this connection, helping the individual to find deeper meaning and align their life with their spiritual beliefs.

The preparation for the healing ritual involves not only the purification of the physical space, but also the mental and emotional preparation of the participant. Meditation and mindfulness practices are useful for calming the mind and focusing intention. The shaman can guide the participant through deep breathing and visualization exercises, creating a state of receptivity for healing.

The ritual itself is a deeply transformative experience. The shaman can begin with an invocation to the guiding spirits and the elements of nature, asking for their presence and assistance in the healing process. The rhythmic sound of the drum or rattle is used to alter the state of consciousness, allowing the shaman and the participant to enter a deep meditative state.

During the spiritual journey, the shaman can meet and interact with animal spirits or ancestral guides. These beings offer wisdom and support, helping to identify the causes of anxiety and stress and to find spiritual solutions to these problems. Communication with these spirits is a vital part of the healing process, providing insights that are not easily accessible in the normal state of consciousness.

The healing energy is channeled through the shaman's hands or through sacred objects such as crystals and feathers. The shaman can direct this energy to specific areas of the body where tension and stress are most pronounced, promoting the release of energy blockages and restoring the flow of vital energy. This practice is often accompanied by chants and mantras that reinforce the healing intention and create an atmosphere of peace and serenity.

Integration is an essential stage after the ritual. The participant is encouraged to reflect on the experience and write down any insights or messages received during the journey. This reflection helps to consolidate the healing and apply the lessons learned in daily life. The shaman can offer additional guidance on how to maintain balance and harmony, suggesting daily practices of meditation, gratitude and connection with nature.

Regular practice of these techniques can help prevent anxiety and stress from returning, promoting a continuous sense of well-being. Creating a sacred space at home, where rituals and meditations can be performed regularly, supports the maintenance of inner peace and energy balance.

Shamanic healing for anxiety and stress offers a holistic and integrated path to well-being. By addressing the underlying causes and promoting healing on all levels of being, the shaman helps the individual to find deep and lasting peace. This approach provides not only relief from symptoms, but also a spiritual transformation that enriches all aspects of life.

The process of shamanic healing for anxiety and stress does not end with the initial ritual. Continuous integration and practical application of the lessons learned during the ritual are crucial to ensuring lasting results. Creating daily routines and practices that support calm and balance is essential to maintain the healing achieved.

One recommended daily practice is meditation. Meditation not only helps to calm the mind, but also strengthens the spiritual connection. Setting aside time every day to sit quietly, concentrating on your breathing and observing your thoughts without judgment, can significantly reduce anxiety and stress. During meditation, visualizing a safe place or a guiding spirit can help reinforce the sense of protection and spiritual guidance.

In addition to meditation, the regular practice of gratitude can have a profound impact on mental and emotional well-being. Keeping a gratitude journal, where you write down three things you are grateful for every day, helps to refocus your mind on positive aspects of life, reducing the tendency to concentrate on worries and stresses. This simple act can transform one's outlook on life, promoting a deeper sense of contentment and peace.

Connecting with nature is another fundamental practice in shamanism. Spending time outdoors, whether walking in a park, sitting by a river or simply watching the sky, can help restore energy balance. Nature has an inherent healing power, and the simple act of being present in a natural environment can recharge vital energy and promote serenity.

Regular purification rituals are equally important. Smoking with sacred herbs, such as sage, can be performed weekly or as needed to cleanse accumulated negative energies. This practice helps to keep the personal space clean and energetically balanced, creating an environment conducive to calm and well-being. Creating an altar with elements of nature and spiritual symbols can serve as a focal point for daily spiritual practice.

The use of mantras and chants can also be incorporated into daily practices. Chanting specific mantras, which resonate with the intention of peace and balance, can help calm the mind and promote healing. Sound has a profound power to alter states of consciousness and realign internal energy, making it a valuable tool in managing anxiety and stress.

The practice of conscious breathing is another effective technique for dealing with anxiety and stress. Breathing exercises, such as diaphragmatic breathing or alternate breathing, help activate the parasympathetic nervous system, promoting a state of deep relaxation. Conscious breathing can be done at any time of the day, especially during moments of high tension, to restore calm and focus.

Community support also plays a crucial role in the healing process. Participating in healing circles or shamanic support groups can provide a sense of belonging and support. Sharing experiences and practices with others who are on the same journey can offer new insights and strengthen the resolve to maintain daily practices.

In addition to these practices, it is important to adopt a compassionate approach to yourself. Anxiety and stress can be significant challenges, and it is essential to recognize one's own efforts and progress along the way. Self-compassion involves treating yourself with kindness and understanding, especially during difficult times, and this can have a profound impact on emotional and spiritual healing.

Finally, the practice of visualizing the intention for healing and balance throughout the day can be a powerful tool. Visualizing a healing light or protective energy around the body can help maintain a state of calm and protection from negative influences. This practice can be carried out anywhere and at any time, continually reinforcing the intention to live in peace and harmony.

Shamanic healing for anxiety and stress is an ongoing process that involves daily practices, self-care and a deep spiritual connection. By integrating these practices into daily life, it is possible to maintain calm, balance and inner peace, facing life's challenges with resilience and serenity.

To deepen the practice of shamanic healing for anxiety and stress, it is essential to understand the importance of symbols and rituals in creating a healing space. These elements are not just decorative; they carry deep meanings and energies that can amplify the effectiveness of spiritual work.

Shamanic symbols, such as mandalas, sacred circles and images of power animals, serve as focal points during meditation and rituals. Mandalas, for example, are geometric representations of the universe and are used to concentrate the mind and enter deep meditative states. Creating a personal mandala can be a meditative activity in itself, helping to clear the mind and set a clear intention for healing.

Sacred circles are another powerful element in shamanic rituals. Representing eternity and the interconnectedness of all things, circles are often used to define ritual space. Drawing a circle on the ground with salt, stones or flowers can create a sacred space where energy is contained and amplified. This space offers spiritual protection and facilitates the connection with guide spirits and the elements of nature.

Power animals are an essential part of shamanic practice. Each animal has unique characteristics and wisdom that can be invoked for guidance and healing. For example, the wolf is often associated with intuition and protection, while the eagle represents vision and freedom. Discovering your power animal can be a journey in itself, carried out through guided meditations or shamanic journeys. Once identified, the power animal can be invoked during rituals to provide strength and support.

Shamanic healing rituals can be enriched with the use of sacred plants. Smoking with herbs such as sage, cedar and palo santo is a common practice to cleanse negative energies and purify the space. These plants have spiritual properties that help raise the vibration of the environment, making it conducive to healing. Preparing a calming herbal tea, such as chamomile or valerian, can complement the practice, providing relaxation and stress relief.

Crystals also play a significant role in healing rituals. Each crystal has a unique vibrational frequency that can be used to balance and harmonize the body's energy. Amethyst, for example, is known for its calming and protective properties, while rose quartz promotes love and inner peace. Placing crystals at strategic points during meditation or ritual can amplify the healing energy.

Music and sound are powerful tools in shamanic practice. The use of drums, rattles and flutes helps induce altered states of consciousness, facilitating the spiritual journey. The steady rhythm of the drum can be particularly effective in calming the mind and promoting introspection. Chants and mantras, repeated rhythmically, also help to concentrate the mind and raise the vibration of the ritual. These sounds create a sacred environment and support healing.

Healing rituals for anxiety and stress can include the creation of a personal altar. This altar serves as a space dedicated to spiritual practice, where symbols, crystals, sacred plants and other meaningful objects can be arranged. Keeping an altar in the home provides a focal point for daily meditation and rituals, continually reminding the intention of healing and spiritual connection. This space should be kept clean and energetically balanced, with regular offerings of flowers, water or incense to honor the spirits and energy of the place.

The practice of visualization is an effective technique to complement shamanic rituals. Visualizing a healing light surrounding the body can help protect against negative energies and promote internal healing. This practice can be integrated into daily meditation, reinforcing the intention of calm and balance. Visualizing a safe place or a spiritual guide can provide comfort and emotional support, especially during times of anxiety.

Shamanic healing is a holistic process that integrates body, mind and spirit. By incorporating sacred symbols, plants, crystals, music and visualizations, it is possible to create powerful rituals that promote deep and lasting healing. Regular practice of these techniques not only relieves anxiety and stress, but also strengthens the spiritual connection, providing an ongoing sense of peace and harmony. By exploring and adopting these practices, each individual can find their own path to healing and balance, living a fuller and more conscious life.

Integrating shamanic practices into daily life is an effective way of maintaining inner peace and emotional balance. A holistic approach to dealing with anxiety and stress involves not only performing periodic rituals, but also adopting habits and attitudes that support ongoing well-being.

One of the most direct ways to apply shamanic principles on a daily basis is through the practice of mindfulness. Mindfulness involves being totally present in the moment, observing thoughts and sensations without judgment. This can be done through short meditations throughout the day or simply by taking a few minutes to breathe deeply and reconnect with the present. The regular practice of mindfulness helps to reduce emotional reactivity and create a space of inner calm.

Connecting with nature is an essential practice in shamanism and can easily be incorporated into the daily routine. Spending time outdoors, whether through hiking, gardening or simply sitting in a park, can have a profound calming effect. Nature is a source of healing and revitalizing energy, and regular interaction with it can help maintain energetic and emotional balance. Taking moments to observe natural cycles, such as sunrise and sunset, can reinforce the feeling of being in tune with the universe.

Another valuable practice is keeping a dream diary. Dreams are seen as a gateway to the unconscious and a way in which spirit guides can communicate. Writing down dreams every morning can help identify patterns, symbols and messages that can be useful for healing and personal growth. The shaman can help interpret these dreams, providing insights into everyday life and emotional challenges.

Creating simple daily rituals can provide structure and meaning to everyday life. These rituals can include lighting a candle and setting an intention for the day, using specific crystals that promote calm and protection, or performing a short morning meditation. These small acts can help start the day with a sense of purpose and spiritual alignment.

The use of herbs and essential oils is another way to support emotional and spiritual health. Plants such as lavender, chamomile and valerian have calming properties and can be used in teas, baths or diffusers. The essential oils of these plants can be applied to pulse points or used in personal inhalers to provide immediate relief from anxiety and stress. Incorporating these practices into your daily routine can create an atmosphere of serenity and well-being.

Practicing gratitude rituals is also key to maintaining a positive state of mind. Taking a moment every day to express gratitude for specific things in life can transform perspective and increase emotional resilience. This ritual can be as simple as verbalizing three things you are grateful for before bed, or writing a letter of gratitude to someone who has had a positive impact. Gratitude helps to focus the mind on the positive and create an attitude of abundance.

Integrating chants and mantras into daily life is an effective way to raise energy vibration and promote calm. Repeating a specific mantra, such as "I am peace" or "I am balance", can help reprogram the mind to desired emotional states. Chanting or reciting mantras during times of stress can create an immediate sense of calm and centeredness.

Practicing art as a spiritual ritual can also be highly beneficial. Activities such as drawing, painting, playing music or dancing allow for emotional expression and the release of accumulated tensions. Art as a spiritual practice is not about creating something perfect, but about allowing energy to flow freely and connecting with the inner self. This creative expression can be a powerful form of healing and self-discovery.

Maintaining a balanced lifestyle, which includes a healthy diet, regular exercise and adequate rest, is essential for general well-being. The shaman can offer guidance on which foods are energetically favorable and which physical activities help maintain the flow of vital energy. A healthy body is the foundation for a peaceful mind and a balanced spirit.

Finally, the continuous search for spiritual knowledge is a practice that supports growth and healing. Reading books on shamanism, attending workshops and seminars, and seeking the guidance of spiritual mentors can enrich the personal journey. Continuous learning and practicing shamanism helps to deepen the connection with guide spirits and expand the understanding of healing practices.

Shamanic healing for anxiety and stress is an ongoing path that involves integrating spiritual practices into daily life. By cultivating habits that promote calm, connection with nature, gratitude and creativity, it is possible to maintain a state of balance and well-being. These practices not only relieve anxiety and stress, but also strengthen the spiritual connection, promoting a fuller and more harmonious life.

Chapter 2
Insomnia

Insomnia is a common problem that affects many people, negatively impacting physical and mental health. It is characterized by difficulty falling asleep, staying asleep or waking up too early, resulting in non-restorative sleep. Lack of adequate sleep can lead to a range of problems, including fatigue, irritability, difficulty concentrating and a general decrease in quality of life.

Identifying the symptoms of insomnia is the first step in addressing this problem. People with insomnia often report being tired but unable to sleep. They may wake up several times during the night or very early in the morning, unable to get back to sleep. This disrupted sleep cycle can create a feeling of constant exhaustion, affecting the ability to function normally during the day.

The causes of insomnia are varied and can include psychological factors such as stress and anxiety, as well as environmental factors such as excessive noise, light or an unsuitable sleeping environment. Other common factors include irregular sleep habits, caffeine or alcohol consumption, and underlying medical conditions such as sleep apnea or chronic pain. Identifying and understanding these causes is crucial to developing an effective healing approach.

The shamanic approach to treating insomnia involves creating an environment conducive to sleep, using relaxation techniques and performing healing rituals to restore energy balance. Preparation for the healing ritual begins with creating a sacred space in the bedroom. This space should be quiet, dark and free of distractions, creating an environment that promotes relaxation and rest.

The space can be purified by burning sacred herbs, such as sage or lavender, which have calming properties. The use of crystals, such as amethyst and rose quartz, can help promote an atmosphere of peace and serenity. Placing these crystals near the bed or under the pillow can help induce a deep, restful sleep.

The shaman can guide the participant through a guided meditation before going to sleep. This meditation can include deep breathing techniques and visualizations that induce a state of deep relaxation. Visualizing a safe and peaceful place, such as a forest or a serene beach, can help calm the mind and prepare the body for sleep. Repeating calming mantras, such as "I am at peace" or "I am safe", can reinforce the feeling of tranquillity.

Shamanic healing rituals can also include the use of calming herbal infusions. Chamomile, valerian or passionflower tea can be taken before bed to relax the body and mind. These herbs have natural sedative properties that can facilitate the onset and maintenance of sleep. Preparing these infusions can be incorporated as an evening ritual, signaling to the body that it's time to rest.

Another effective practice is the use of music or nature sounds to induce sleep. Soft sounds, such as the murmur of a stream or the singing of birds, can create a relaxing environment that helps the mind disconnect from daily worries. There are specific recordings of shamanic music or nature sounds that can be used during the night to promote deep, restorative sleep.

The alignment of circadian rhythms is crucial for a good quality of sleep. Keeping a regular schedule for going to sleep and waking up helps to regulate the internal biological clock. Avoiding stimulants such as caffeine and electronics in the hours before sleep is also important to prepare the body and mind for rest. The shaman can suggest routine practices, such as taking a hot bath or reading a calming book, to signal to the body that it's time to sleep.

The practice of relaxation techniques, such as gentle stretching or yoga, can be integrated into the evening routine. These exercises help to release tension built up in the muscles and calm the mind. Specific yoga poses, such as the child's pose or the bridge pose, are particularly effective for promoting relaxation and preparing the body for sleep.

Shamanic healing for insomnia involves a set of holistic practices that address both the underlying causes and the symptoms. By creating an environment conducive to sleep, using relaxation techniques and performing healing rituals, it is possible to restore energy balance and promote deep, restorative sleep. These practices not only relieve insomnia, but also improve the overall quality of life, providing refreshing rest and enhanced mental and physical health.

Understanding the underlying causes of insomnia is crucial to addressing it effectively. Often, insomnia is a symptom of deeper imbalances, whether on an emotional, mental or spiritual level. Shamanism offers powerful tools to identify and treat these imbalances, promoting restorative sleep and holistic health.

Emotional causes of insomnia can include chronic stress, anxiety, and unresolved trauma. The mind can be overloaded with worries and fears, making it difficult to relax enough to fall asleep. To address these causes, it is important to create a safe space where emotions can be expressed and released. The shaman can guide the participant on a shamanic journey to explore and understand these emotions, helping to identify and release the emotional blockages that prevent restful sleep.

Mental problems, such as obsessive thoughts or a fast mental pace, can also contribute to insomnia. The mind can be so active that it can't switch off at bedtime. Meditation and mindfulness practices are effective for calming the mind. Guided meditation before bed can include visualizations of peaceful settings, such as a forest or a beach, where the participant can feel safe and relaxed. Deep breathing techniques, such as the 4-7-8 breath (inhale for 4 seconds, hold for 7 seconds and exhale for 8 seconds), help to slow down the mental rhythm and prepare the body for sleep.

The spiritual causes of insomnia can involve a disconnection with one's purpose in life or with one's spirituality. Feeling lost or without direction can create a deep restlessness that manifests as insomnia. The shaman can help the participant reconnect with their spirituality through rituals and ceremonies that reinforce the connection with spirit guides and nature. Creating an altar in the home, with symbols that represent personal spirituality, can serve as a constant reminder of this connection and help create an environment conducive to sleep.

The sleeping environment is a crucial factor in combating insomnia. A bedroom that promotes relaxation should be dark, quiet and comfortable. Investing in blackout curtains, earplugs and a quality mattress can make a big difference to the quality of sleep. Keeping the bedroom at a pleasant temperature and free of electronics is also important. The presence of blue light from electronic devices can interfere with the production of melatonin, the hormone that regulates sleep. Switching off these devices at least an hour before bedtime can help prepare the body for rest.

Using nightly rituals can signal to the body that it's time to prepare for sleep. A warm bath before bed can help relax the muscles and calm the mind. Adding a few drops of lavender essential oil to the bath can enhance this effect, due to its calming properties. After bathing, practicing a personal care routine, such as brushing your teeth and applying soothing lotions or oils, can create a sense of routine and predictability, helping the body to prepare for sleep.

Practicing gratitude before bed is a powerful technique for transforming your mindset and promoting restful sleep. Taking a few minutes to reflect on the things you are grateful for can change the focus of your mind from worries to positive feelings. Writing down three things you are grateful for at the end of the day can create a mental state of contentment and peace, making it easier to fall asleep.

The shamanic journey can be used specifically to treat insomnia. During the journey, the shaman can seek guidance from the guide spirits about the causes of insomnia and the appropriate healing methods. The spirit guides can offer valuable insights and help restore energetic balance. After the journey, the shaman can share these messages with the participant and suggest specific practices to integrate these insights into the daily routine.

Sleep recovery can be a gradual process. It's important to be patient and continue practicing the recommended techniques, even if the results aren't immediate. Consistency is the key to establishing new sleep patterns. Keeping a sleep diary, where you record your sleep habits and nightly practices, can help you identify patterns and adjust your practices as necessary.

Once the underlying causes of insomnia have been identified and the sleep environment has been prepared, it is essential to incorporate specific shamanic healing techniques that help relieve insomnia effectively. These techniques include performing night rituals, using medicinal plants and integrating visualization and meditation practices that promote relaxation and tranquility.

Preparing for a healing ritual begins with setting a clear intention. Intention is the basis of any spiritual practice and helps to direct healing energy effectively. Before starting the ritual, take a moment to reflect on your intention to achieve deep, restful sleep. Writing this intention on a piece of paper and placing it on the altar can help focus the mind and energize the sacred space.

Purification rituals are fundamental to creating a clean and energetically balanced environment. Smoking with sacred herbs, such as sage or palo santo, can be done in the bedroom before going to sleep. The smoke from these herbs helps to cleanse negative energies and prepare the room for rest. When carrying out the fumigation, move slowly around the room, concentrating on specific areas that can accumulate stagnant energy, such as corners or under the bed.

Creating a personal altar can serve as a focal point for night rituals. This altar can include healing crystals, candles, and symbols that represent the intention of restful sleep. Crystals such as amethyst, known for its calming properties, and rose quartz, which promotes inner peace, can be placed on the altar or under the pillow. Soft candlelight also helps to create a peaceful and relaxing atmosphere.

The use of medicinal plants is a traditional practice in shamanism and can be especially effective in treating insomnia. Herbal teas such as chamomile, valerian and passionflower are known for their natural sedative properties. Drinking a cup of chamomile tea before bed can help calm the mind and relax the body. Preparing and consuming this tea can be part of an evening ritual that signals to the body that it's time to rest.

The practice of visualization is a powerful technique for inducing sleep. When you lie down, close your eyes and imagine a safe and peaceful place. It could be a serene forest, a secluded beach or any place where you feel at peace. Visualize yourself walking there, feeling the gentle breeze and listening to the sounds of nature. This practice helps to take your mind off your daily worries and create a state of deep relaxation.

Guided meditations are another effective tool for combating insomnia. There are many recordings of guided meditations available designed specifically for falling asleep. These meditations usually include breathing instructions, visualizations and calming affirmations. Choose a meditation that resonates with you and listen to it as you prepare for sleep. Regular repetition of this practice can help train your mind and body to relax and fall asleep more easily.

Shamanic mantras and chants can also be incorporated into the nighttime routine. Repeating a calming mantra, such as "I am peace" or "I am safe", can help calm the mind and induce a state of tranquillity. Soft chants can be sung while getting ready for bed, helping to establish an atmosphere of peace and serenity. These vibrational sounds help to align the body's energy and prepare the mind for rest.

The practice of conscious breathing is crucial to relieving insomnia. Breathing techniques, such as diaphragmatic breathing or the 4-7-8 technique, help to calm the nervous system and prepare the body for sleep. Diaphragmatic breathing involves breathing deeply through the nose, expanding the abdomen, and exhaling slowly through the mouth. The 4-7-8 technique consists of breathing in for 4 seconds, holding the breath for 7 seconds and breathing out slowly for 8 seconds. These practices can be done while lying in bed, helping to induce a state of deep relaxation.

Integrating self-compassion and acceptance practices is essential. Recognizing that insomnia can be a challenge and treating yourself with kindness and understanding can relieve the pressure of trying to sleep. Accepting that some nights may be more difficult than others and practicing patience with yourself is an important part of the healing journey.

Shamanic healing for insomnia involves the integration of holistic techniques and practices that promote relaxation and energy balance. By creating an environment conducive to sleep, performing purification rituals, using medicinal plants and incorporating visualization and meditation practices, it is possible to combat insomnia effectively. These practices not only help to improve the quality of sleep, but also promote general well-being, leading to a more balanced and harmonious life.

To complement nighttime practices and healing rituals, it is essential to incorporate daytime activities and habits that support healthy sleep. Integrating daily practices that promote balance and stress reduction can help prepare the body and mind for restful sleep at night.

A fundamental aspect of shamanic healing is the continuous connection with nature. Spending time outdoors, especially during the day, can have a significant impact on sleep quality. Exposure to natural sunlight helps regulate the circadian rhythm, the body's biological cycle of sleep and wakefulness. Dedicating at least 20 to 30 minutes a day to sunlight, preferably in the morning, can help synchronize the biological clock and improve melatonin production at night.

Regular physical exercise also plays a crucial role in promoting healthy sleep. Activities such as walking, running, yoga or tai chi not only help to reduce stress and anxiety, but also prepare the body for a deeper rest. However, it is important to avoid intense exercise in the hours before sleep, as this can increase adrenaline levels and make it difficult to fall asleep.

Diet also influences the quality of sleep. A balanced diet, rich in nutrients and low in caffeine and refined sugars, can promote a more restful sleep. Foods rich in tryptophan, such as bananas, nuts and seeds, help increase the production of serotonin, a precursor to melatonin. Avoiding heavy and stimulating meals, such as coffee and chocolate, in the hours before sleep can help prepare the body for rest.

Gratitude rituals are powerful daytime practices that can positively influence sleep. Taking a moment throughout the day to reflect on the things you are grateful for can help refocus your mind on positive aspects of life, reducing stress and promoting a sense of contentment. Keeping a gratitude journal, where you write down three things you are grateful for every day, can create a more relaxed and receptive state of mind for sleep.

Spiritual connection is another essential practice for promoting healthy sleep. Taking part in regular shamanic ceremonies, whether in a group or individually, can help maintain spiritual and emotional harmony. These rituals provide an opportunity to release accumulated negative energies and strengthen the connection with the guiding spirits. The practice of meditation and prayer throughout the day can strengthen this connection and prepare the mind for a peaceful rest.

The use of healing crystals during the day can also support the quality of sleep at night. Crystals such as amethyst and sodalite can be carried in the pocket or worn as jewelry to promote calm and mental clarity. Placing these crystals under the pillow or next to the bed can help create an energetic environment that favors restful sleep.

Practicing conscious breathing throughout the day can help reduce tension and anxiety, preparing the body for a restful sleep. Simple breathing exercises, such as inhaling deeply through the nose and exhaling slowly through the mouth, can be done at any time to calm the nervous system. The 4-7-8 breathing technique is particularly effective for inducing relaxation and can be practiced before bed or during times of stress.

The art of creating a daily routine that supports healthy sleep involves integrating various practices and habits that promote general well-being. Maintaining regular bedtimes and wake-up times, even at weekends, helps to regulate the circadian rhythm. Establishing a relaxing evening routine, which includes activities such as reading a calming book, taking a warm bath or practicing gentle yoga, signals the body that it's time to prepare for sleep.

Practicing positive visualizations during the day can also influence the quality of sleep. Visualizing peaceful and pleasant scenarios, such as a walk in the woods or a day at the beach, can help reduce stress and anxiety, preparing the mind for a deeper rest at night. These visualizations can be integrated into meditation practice or carried out while lying in bed, waiting to fall asleep.

Finally, it is important to cultivate an attitude of acceptance and patience with yourself when dealing with insomnia. Recognize that the journey to better sleep can take time and that each step, however small, is progress towards better well-being. Treating yourself with kindness and compassion, and celebrating small victories, can take the pressure off and promote a more relaxed and positive mindset.

Shamanic healing for insomnia is a holistic process that involves integrating daytime and nighttime practices that promote balance and harmony. By adopting healthy habits, spiritual practices and relaxation techniques, it is possible to create an environment conducive to sleep and significantly improve the quality of rest. These practices not only help combat insomnia, but also promote general well-being, providing a fuller and more harmonious life.

The journey to curing insomnia through shamanism is an ongoing process that involves integrating various holistic practices into your daily life. In addition to the techniques mentioned above, it is essential to incorporate strategies that promote continued healing and the maintenance of healthy sleep. These strategies include keeping a sleep diary, practicing full and new moon rituals, and using protective visualizations during the night.

Keeping a sleep diary can be a powerful tool for identifying patterns and improving sleep quality. This diary should include notes on bedtimes and wake times, sleep quality, dreams, and any events or thoughts that may have impacted sleep. Reviewing these notes regularly can help identify factors that contribute to insomnia and develop strategies to address them. The sleep diary can also serve as a record of progress and the practices that work best, providing a clear vision of the path to healing.

The practice of full and new moon rituals is a shamanic tradition that can be particularly effective for promoting sleep and energy renewal. The full moon is a time to release what no longer serves, while the new moon is a time to plant new intentions and start afresh. During the full moon, the shaman can guide the participant in a release ritual, where they write on a piece of paper all the worries, fears and negative energies that need to be left behind. Burning this paper in a fire or with a candle can symbolize the release of these energies. During the new moon, the shaman can guide the setting of new intentions for sleep and well-being by writing them down and keeping them on the personal altar.

The use of protective visualizations can help to create a safe and peaceful environment for sleep. Before going to sleep, the participant can visualize a protective light around their body and their room, forming a barrier against negative energies. This light can be visualized as a specific color, such as white or gold, which symbolizes protection and peace. Reinforcing this visualization with the repetition of protective mantras, such as "I am safe and protected", can strengthen the feeling of security and promote a more peaceful sleep.

Practicing gratitude rituals when you wake up can also positively influence the quality of your sleep. Starting the day with a moment of gratitude helps to set a positive tone and cultivate a mindset of abundance. This practice can include giving thanks for a restful sleep, for the opportunity of a new day and for any other positive aspect of life. Keeping a gratitude journal where you record these thoughts can serve as a constant reminder of the positive, reducing the stress and anxiety that can affect sleep.

Integrating self-care practices during the day can support sleep quality at night. This includes dedicating time to activities that promote relaxation and happiness, such as hobbies, light physical exercise, and quality time with loved ones. Practicing self-care helps to balance emotions and reduce stress, creating a solid foundation for restful sleep.

In addition, it is important to be aware of the consumption of substances that can interfere with sleep, such as caffeine, alcohol and heavy foods close to bedtime. Opting for a balanced diet and avoiding these stimulants in the hours before sleep can significantly improve the quality of your rest. Including foods rich in magnesium and tryptophan, such as nuts, seeds and bananas, can help promote muscle relaxation and induce sleep.

Practicing grounding exercises can also be beneficial. This involves connecting directly with the earth, whether by walking barefoot on the grass, sitting on the earth or meditating outdoors. Grounding helps to balance the body's energy and reduce stress, promoting a sense of calm and stability that can facilitate sleep.

The shamanic journey to cure insomnia is an ongoing process that requires patience, dedication and the integration of various holistic practices. By creating an environment conducive to sleep, practicing rituals of release and intention, and adopting daily habits that promote well-being, it is possible to combat insomnia in an effective and lasting way. These practices not only help to improve the quality of sleep, but also promote holistic health, providing a more balanced and harmonious life. By continuing to explore and integrate these practices, each individual can find their own path to healing and restful sleep.

Chapter 3
Depression

Depression is a mental health condition that affects millions of people worldwide, profoundly impacting quality of life and well-being. It is characterized by persistent feelings of sadness, hopelessness and a lack of interest or pleasure in daily activities. Understanding the nature of depression and its causes is the first step towards addressing this condition effectively through shamanic practices.

The symptoms of depression vary from person to person, but often include feelings of intense sadness, loss of interest in previously pleasurable activities, changes in appetite and sleep, fatigue, difficulty concentrating, feelings of guilt or worthlessness and thoughts of death or suicide. These symptoms can be debilitating, affecting a person's ability to function on a daily basis and maintain healthy relationships.

The causes of depression are complex and can involve a combination of biological, psychological and social factors. Chemical imbalances in the brain, past trauma, chronic stress, loss of a loved one, interpersonal conflicts and physical health problems can all contribute to the development of depression. Shamanism offers a holistic approach to healing, which considers all these aspects and seeks to restore balance and harmony in the individual.

Preparation for the shamanic treatment of depression begins with the creation of a safe and sacred space where the healing process can take place. This space should be quiet and free of distractions, allowing for a deep connection with the spiritual world. Purification of the space can be done by burning sacred herbs, such as sage or cedar, to cleanse negative energies and prepare the environment for healing.

Creating a personal altar is an important step. This altar can include elements that symbolize the healing intention, such as crystals, candles, plants and spiritual symbols. Crystals such as amethyst, which promotes calm and peace, and citrine, which helps elevate mood and energy, can be used on the altar. Soft candlelight can help create an atmosphere of serenity and introspection.

Shamanic journeying is a powerful technique for treating depression. During the journey, the shaman enters an altered state of consciousness to connect with guide spirits and gain insights into the causes of depression and appropriate healing methods. The journey can be guided by the rhythmic sound of the drum or rattle, which helps induce a deep meditative state. The shaman can meet and interact with animal spirits or ancestral guides, who offer wisdom and support.

Shamanic healing rituals for depression can include the recovery of parts of the soul. Depression often results from past traumas that fragment the soul, leaving the person feeling incomplete or disconnected. The shaman works to recover these lost parts of the soul, reintegrating them into the individual and restoring fullness and vitality. This process can be accompanied by chants and mantras that reinforce the intention of healing and reconnection.

The use of medicinal plants is a traditional practice in shamanism and can be particularly effective in treating depression. Herbs such as St. John's wort, lavender and chamomile have properties that help relieve the symptoms of depression and promote calm and relaxation. Teas from these herbs can be consumed daily as part of a healing ritual.

Meditation and visualization are essential tools for combating depression. Guided meditations that focus on visualizing light and healing can help transform negative energy and promote a state of inner peace. Visualizing a golden or white light entering the body and filling every cell with healing and love can be a powerful practice for lifting mood and restoring hope.

Conscious breathing exercises are also effective in relieving the symptoms of depression. The practice of deep, controlled breathing can help calm the nervous system and reduce the anxiety associated with depression. Techniques such as 4-7-8 breathing (inhale for 4 seconds, hold for 7 seconds and exhale slowly for 8 seconds) can be performed several times a day to promote calm and balance.

Community support is a crucial aspect in the process of healing from depression. Participating in healing circles or shamanic support groups can provide a sense of belonging and emotional support. Sharing experiences and practices with others who are on the same journey can offer new insights and strengthen the determination to move forward.

In addition to these practices, it is important to cultivate an attitude of self-compassion and acceptance. Recognizing that depression is a medical condition that requires care and treatment, and treating yourself with kindness and understanding, is fundamental to healing. Regular practice of self-compassion can help alleviate feelings of guilt or worthlessness and promote a sense of self-acceptance and self-love.

Shamanic healing for depression involves a holistic approach that considers all aspects of being - physical, emotional, mental and spiritual. By creating an environment conducive to healing, carrying out shamanic journeys, using medicinal plants, and incorporating meditation and breathing practices, it is possible to treat depression in an effective and lasting way. These practices not only help relieve the symptoms of depression, but also promote holistic health, providing a more balanced and harmonious life.

Emotional trauma is one of the main causes of depression. Painful experiences from the past, such as the loss of loved ones, abuse or rejection, can leave deep scars. These traumatic experiences can fragment the soul, creating a feeling of emptiness and disconnection. The practice of soul retrieval is a powerful shamanic technique that aims to reintegrate lost parts of the soul, promoting healing and a sense of completeness. During the shamanic journey, the shaman searches for these fragmented parts of the soul in the spiritual realms and brings them back to the individual, restoring wholeness and vitality.

Internal conflicts, such as feelings of guilt, shame and low self-esteem, can also contribute to depression. These conflicts often result from negative beliefs about oneself, often internalized over time. The shaman can work with the individual to identify these limiting beliefs and transform them. Using visualization and affirmation techniques, it is possible to replace negative thoughts with positive ones, promoting self-acceptance and self-love.

Spiritual disconnection is another significant factor that can lead to depression. Feeling disconnected from one's purpose in life or from a greater force can create a sense of emptiness and hopelessness. Shamanic practice involves reconnecting with the spiritual world and nature, helping the individual to find meaning and purpose. Performing rituals of gratitude and connection with the elements of nature can help restore this connection. Spending time outdoors, meditating in natural places and making offerings to the earth are all practices that can strengthen the spiritual connection and promote healing.

The use of medicinal plants remains a fundamental practice in the shamanic treatment of depression. Herbs such as St. John's wort, known for its antidepressant properties, and lavender, which promotes calm, can be integrated into the daily routine. Drinking teas from these herbs or using essential oils in diffusers can help relieve the symptoms of depression. In addition, creating a medicinal herb garden can be a therapeutic activity that connects the individual to the earth and promotes well-being.

Creating a sacred environment at home is crucial to supporting the healing process. Maintaining a space dedicated to spiritual practice, such as an altar, can serve as a focal point for meditation and daily rituals. This space should be kept clean and energetically balanced, with the regular burning of sacred herbs for purification. Including elements of nature, such as stones, shells and plants, can help create an atmosphere of serenity and connection.

The practice of meditation and visualization is essential for treating depression. Guided meditations involving visualizations of light and healing can help transform negative energies and promote a state of inner peace. Visualizing a golden or white light entering the body and filling every cell with healing and love can be a powerful practice for lifting mood and restoring hope. This practice can be done daily, upon waking or before going to sleep, to reinforce the intention of healing.

Conscious breathing exercises are equally important. Regular practice of deep, controlled breathing can help calm the nervous system and reduce the anxiety associated with depression. Techniques such as diaphragmatic breathing or alternate breathing can be performed several times a day to promote calm and balance. These practices can be incorporated into the daily routine, during times of stress or as part of a morning or evening ritual.

Participating in healing circles or shamanic support groups can provide a sense of community and emotional support. These groups offer a safe space to share experiences and practices, and to receive support from others who are on the same healing journey. The exchange of wisdom and healing techniques can offer new insights and strengthen the resolve to move forward. The feeling of belonging and connection with others can be a powerful antidote to the sense of isolation that often accompanies depression.

Shamanic healing for depression involves a holistic approach that considers all aspects of being - physical, emotional, mental and spiritual. By creating an environment conducive to healing, carrying out shamanic journeys, using medicinal plants, and incorporating meditation and breathing practices, it is possible to treat depression in an effective and lasting way. These practices not only help relieve the symptoms of depression, but also promote holistic health, providing a more balanced and harmonious life.

A holistic approach to healing depression involves integrating shamanic practices into the daily routine, complemented by rituals and techniques that promote emotional and spiritual balance. Continuing from the previously mentioned practices, delving into specific healing techniques can offer ongoing support for those struggling with depression.

Shamanic healing rituals for depression include the use of specific chants and mantras that promote the upliftment of the spirit and the renewal of energy. Traditional shamanic chants, which are passed down from generation to generation, carry vibrations that can help release negative energies and bring inner peace. Repeating mantras such as "I am light" or "I am love" can reinforce positive feelings and dispel negative thoughts. These chants and mantras can be chanted daily, especially at dawn and dusk, to set a positive tone for the day and night.

Practicing art therapy is another effective technique for treating depression. Artistic activities, such as drawing, painting or creating mandalas, allow for emotional expression and the release of internal tensions. The creative process can be a form of meditation, where the mind calms down and focuses on the present moment. Creating art inspired by themes of healing and transformation can help channel difficult emotions and promote a sense of fulfillment and purpose.

Ritual baths are a traditional practice in shamanism that can be used for purification and energy renewal. Preparing a bath with sacred herbs such as lavender, rosemary and chamomile can help relax the body and mind. Adding a few drops of lavender or eucalyptus essential oil can increase the calming effect. During the bath, visualizing the water cleansing all negative energies and bringing a feeling of renewal and peace can be a powerful practice. This ritual can be performed weekly or as needed, especially during times of intense stress or sadness.

Practicing grounding exercises is essential for those suffering from depression. Grounding involves connecting directly with the earth, whether by walking barefoot on the grass, sitting on the earth or meditating outdoors. This practice helps to balance the body's energy and reduce stress, promoting a sense of calm and stability. Direct contact with nature can re-energize and revitalize, helping to relieve depression and restore emotional balance.

Creating a healing journal is a valuable tool for tracking progress and reflecting on the healing journey. This journal can include daily notes on feelings and thoughts, as well as records of dreams and insights received during meditations or shamanic journeys. Keeping a record of rituals performed, herbs and crystals used, and experiences with chants and mantras can help identify patterns and adjust practices as necessary. The healing journal serves as a safe space to express emotions and document the path to recovery.

The practice of yoga and gentle stretching can complement shamanic techniques, helping to release physical and emotional tension. Specific yoga postures, such as child's pose and warrior's pose, promote relaxation and inner strength. Regular yoga practice can help balance the chakras, the body's energy centers, and promote a general sense of well-being. Incorporating breathing and meditation techniques during yoga practice can intensify the healing effects.

Gratitude rituals remain a fundamental practice for combating depression. Taking a moment throughout the day to reflect on the things you are grateful for can help refocus the mind on positive aspects of life, reducing stress and promoting a sense of contentment. Keeping a gratitude journal, where you write down three things you are grateful for every day, can create a more relaxed and receptive state of mind. This simple act can transform one's outlook on life and promote a deeper sense of peace and harmony.

Participation in healing circles or shamanic support groups remains a crucial aspect of the healing process. These groups offer a safe space to share experiences and practices, and to receive support from others who are on the same journey. The exchange of wisdom and healing techniques can offer new insights and strengthen the determination to move forward. The feeling of belonging and connection with others can be a powerful antidote to the sense of isolation that often accompanies depression.

Shamanic healing for depression involves a holistic approach that considers all aspects of being - physical, emotional, mental and spiritual. By creating an environment conducive to healing, carrying out shamanic journeys, using medicinal plants, and incorporating meditation and breathing practices, it is possible to treat depression in an effective and lasting way. These practices not only help relieve the symptoms of depression, but also promote holistic health, providing a more balanced and harmonious life.

The shamanic approach to curing depression also includes the integration of mindfulness practices, which can be incorporated into the daily routine to promote emotional and mental balance. In addition, the performance of spiritual connection rituals and the use of self-care techniques are fundamental to sustaining the healing process.

The practice of mindfulness involves being fully present in the moment, observing thoughts and emotions without judgment. This can be particularly useful for people struggling with depression, helping them to break the cycle of rumination and focus on the here and now. Daily mindfulness meditations can include observing the breath, listening to the sounds around you or paying full attention to bodily sensations. These practices can be done in short sessions throughout the day, helping to create a continuous state of awareness and presence.

Spiritual connection rituals are a central part of shamanism and can be used to strengthen the connection with the divine and with one's life purpose. One powerful practice is invoking guardian spirits and ancestors to ask for guidance and protection. This can be done through prayers, chants or simple intentions spoken aloud. Creating a sacred space where these invocations can be made regularly helps to establish a spiritual routine and foster a sense of spiritual connection and support.

Integrating self-care practices is essential for maintaining emotional and mental well-being. This can include activities that bring joy and satisfaction, such as hobbies, light physical exercise, quality time with loved ones and moments of rest and relaxation. Self-care also involves attention to physical health, with a balanced and adequate diet, hydration and sufficient sleep. Practices such as self-massage with essential oils, relaxing baths and creating a comfortable and welcoming environment at home can make a big difference to overall well-being.

Shamanic healing rituals for depression can also include practicing gratitude and celebrating small daily victories. Gratitude helps to shift the mind's focus from negative to positive aspects of life. Taking a moment each evening to reflect on three things you are grateful for can transform your perspective and promote a more positive mindset. This ritual can be carried out as part of the nightly routine, helping to prepare the mind for a more peaceful and restful sleep.

Another effective technique is the creation of mandalas, which are spiritual symbols used for meditation and healing. Drawing or painting mandalas can be a meditative practice that helps calm the mind and promote introspection. Mandalas can be created with the intention of healing and transformation, using colors and shapes that resonate with the desired energy. This creative process can help release repressed emotions and find a sense of balance and harmony.

The practice of guided visualizations is a powerful technique for combating depression. Visualizations that involve healing scenarios and light can help transform negative energies and promote a state of inner peace. Visualizing a golden or white light entering the body and filling every cell with healing and love can be a powerful daily practice. This visualization can be done during meditation, before bed or at times of need during the day.

Conscious breathing exercises are equally important for promoting calm and reducing the anxiety associated with depression. Techniques such as diaphragmatic breathing or alternate breathing can be practiced regularly to calm the nervous system and promote a sense of relaxation. These practices can be integrated into the daily routine, helping to create a foundation of calm and balance.

Participating in healing circles or shamanic support groups remains a crucial aspect of the healing process. These groups offer a safe space to share experiences and practices, and to receive support from others who are on the same journey. The exchange of wisdom and healing techniques can offer new insights and strengthen the determination to move forward. The feeling of belonging and connection with others can be a powerful antidote to the sense of isolation that often accompanies depression.

The integration of vibrational healing techniques, such as the use of Tibetan bowls and bells, can complement other shamanic practices. The sound of these tools can help balance the body's energy and promote a state of calm and serenity. Using these instruments during meditations or healing rituals can intensify the healing effects and promote general well-being.

Shamanic healing for depression involves a holistic approach that considers all aspects of the being - physical, emotional, mental and spiritual. By creating an environment conducive to healing, carrying out shamanic journeys, using medicinal plants, and incorporating meditation and breathing practices, it is possible to treat depression in an effective and lasting way. These practices not only help relieve the symptoms of depression, but also promote holistic health, providing a more balanced and harmonious life.

Shamanic practice offers a comprehensive approach to healing depression, integrating spiritual, emotional and physical techniques that promote holistic well-being. In addition to the practices already discussed, there are several other techniques and rituals that can be incorporated into the daily routine to support ongoing healing and strengthen emotional resilience.

The practice of gratitude is a powerful technique that can transform one's outlook on life and promote feelings of well-being and contentment. Taking a moment every day to reflect on the things you are grateful for helps refocus the mind on positive aspects of life, reducing stress and promoting a sense of abundance. Keeping a gratitude journal, where you write down three things you are grateful for every day, can create a more relaxed and receptive state of mind. This simple act can transform one's outlook on life and promote a deeper sense of peace and harmony.

Practicing grounding exercises is essential for those suffering from depression. Grounding involves connecting directly with the earth, whether by walking barefoot on the grass, sitting on the earth or meditating outdoors. This practice helps to balance the body's energy and reduce stress, promoting a sense of calm and stability. Direct contact with nature can re-energize and revitalize, helping to relieve depression and restore emotional balance.

The use of healing crystals is a traditional practice in shamanism and can be particularly effective in treating depression. Crystals such as amethyst, known for its calming properties, and citrine, which helps elevate mood and energy, can be worn on the altar or carried in the pocket during the day. Placing these crystals under the pillow or next to the bed can help create an energetic environment that favors restful sleep and emotional healing.

Shamanic healing rituals can also include the practice of positive visualizations. Visualizing peaceful and pleasant scenarios, such as a walk in a forest or a day at the beach, can help reduce stress and anxiety, preparing the mind for a deeper rest at night. These visualizations can be integrated into meditation practice or carried out while lying in bed, waiting to fall asleep. The regular practice of visualizations can help create a sense of peace and serenity, promoting a more positive mindset.

Regular physical exercise is crucial for promoting healthy sleep and reducing symptoms of depression. Activities such as walking, running, yoga or tai chi not only help to reduce stress and anxiety, but also prepare the body for a deeper rest. However, it is important to avoid intense exercise in the hours before sleep, as this can increase adrenaline levels and make it difficult to fall asleep. The practice of yoga and gentle stretching can complement shamanic techniques, helping to release physical and emotional tension. Specific yoga postures, such as child's pose and warrior's pose, promote relaxation and inner strength.

Practicing art as a form of therapy can also be highly beneficial in combating depression. Activities such as drawing, painting or sculpting allow for emotional expression and the release of internal tensions. The creative process can be a form of meditation, where the mind calms down and focuses on the present moment. Creating art inspired by themes of healing and transformation can help channel difficult emotions and find a sense of fulfillment and purpose.

Participation in healing circles or shamanic support groups remains a crucial aspect of the healing process. These groups offer a safe space to share experiences and practices, and to receive support from others who are on the same journey. The exchange of wisdom and healing techniques can offer new insights and strengthen the determination to move forward. The feeling of belonging and connection with others can be a powerful antidote to the sense of isolation that often accompanies depression.

Practicing guided meditations that involve visualizations of light and healing can help transform negative energies and promote a state of inner peace. Visualizing a golden or white light entering the body and filling every cell with healing and love can be a powerful daily practice.

This visualization can be done during meditation, before bed or in times of need during the day. Conscious breathing exercises are equally important for promoting calm and reducing the anxiety associated with depression. Techniques such as diaphragmatic breathing or alternate breathing can be practiced regularly to calm the nervous system and promote a sense of relaxation.

Finally, it is important to adopt an attitude of self-compassion and patience during the healing process. Recognizing that depression is a complex condition that requires time and care to treat is fundamental. Treating yourself with kindness and understanding, and celebrating small progress, can take the pressure off and promote a more positive mindset. Regularly practicing self-compassion can help relieve feelings of guilt or worthlessness and promote a sense of self-acceptance and self-love.

Shamanic healing for depression involves a holistic approach that considers all aspects of being - physical, emotional, mental and spiritual. By creating an environment conducive to healing, carrying out shamanic journeys, using medicinal plants, and incorporating meditation and breathing practices, it is possible to treat depression in an effective and lasting way. These practices not only help to alleviate the symptoms of depression, but also promote holistic health, providing a more balanced and harmonious life.

Chapter 4
Emotional Blocks

Emotional blockages are internal barriers that prevent the natural flow of emotions and can have a significant impact on a person's life. These blockages can result from past traumas, painful experiences, or simply the prolonged suppression of feelings. They can manifest as difficulties in expressing emotions, feeling empathy, or connecting with others on a deep level. The shamanic approach offers various techniques for identifying and releasing these blockages, promoting an emotionally balanced and healthy life.

Symptoms of emotional blockages can vary, but often include a feeling of emotional numbness, difficulties in forming and maintaining relationships, feelings of isolation, and disproportionate emotional responses to everyday situations. These blockages can interfere with a person's ability to experience joy, love and compassion, negatively affecting their quality of life and general well-being.

Identifying the underlying causes of emotional blockages is the first step in addressing them. Often, these blockages are rooted in unresolved emotional traumas, such as abuse, loss, rejection or experiences of shame. The shaman works to explore and understand these causes, using techniques such as shamanic journeying to access repressed memories and emotions. During the journey, the shaman enters an altered state of consciousness to connect with guide spirits and gain insights into the origins of emotional blockages.

The creation of a sacred space is fundamental to the healing process. This space should be quiet and free of distractions, allowing for a deep connection with the spiritual world. The space can be purified by burning sacred herbs, such as sage or cedar, to cleanse negative energies and prepare the environment for healing. Creating a personal altar, with elements that symbolize the intention of emotional healing, such as crystals, candles and plants, can help focus the energy and intention.

Healing crystals are powerful tools in shamanic practice and can be used to release emotional blockages. Crystals such as rose quartz, known for promoting love and compassion, and amethyst, which helps calm the mind and relieve stress, can be used during meditations and healing rituals. Placing these crystals on the altar or carrying them with you during the day can help keep the focus on emotional healing.

Shamanic healing rituals for emotional blockages can include the use of specific chants and mantras that promote the release of repressed emotions and reconnection with feelings of love and compassion. Traditional shamanic chants, which are passed down from generation to generation, carry vibrations that can help release negative energies and bring inner peace. Repeating mantras such as "I am love" or "I release and forgive" can reinforce positive feelings and help dissolve emotional blockages.

Practicing art therapy is another effective technique for treating emotional blockages. Artistic activities, such as drawing, painting or creating mandalas, allow for emotional expression and the release of internal tensions. The creative process can be a form of meditation, where the mind calms down and focuses on the present moment. Creating art inspired by themes of healing and transformation can help channel difficult emotions and find a sense of fulfillment and purpose.

Conscious breathing exercises are equally important for promoting calm and reducing the anxiety associated with emotional blockages. Regular practice of deep, controlled breathing can help calm the nervous system and promote a sense of relaxation. Techniques such as diaphragmatic breathing or alternate breathing can be performed several times a day to release emotional tension and promote calm.

Integrating mindfulness practices into daily routines can help promote emotional awareness and avoid suppressing feelings. Mindfulness involves being fully present in the moment, observing thoughts and emotions without judgment. This practice can help break the cycle of rumination and create a space for healthy emotional expression. Daily mindfulness meditations can include observing the breath, listening to the sounds around you or paying full attention to bodily sensations.

Participation in healing circles or shamanic support groups can provide a sense of community and emotional support. These groups offer a safe space to share experiences and practices, and to receive support from others who are on the same healing journey. The exchange of wisdom and healing techniques can offer new insights and strengthen the resolve to move forward. The feeling of belonging and connection with others can be a powerful antidote to the sense of isolation that often accompanies emotional blockages.

Shamanic healing for emotional blockages involves a holistic approach that considers all aspects of being - physical, emotional, mental and spiritual. By creating an environment conducive to healing, carrying out shamanic journeys, using healing crystals and incorporating meditation and breathing practices, it is possible to treat emotional blockages in an effective and lasting way. These practices not only help to relieve the symptoms of emotional blockages, but also promote holistic health, providing a more balanced and harmonious life.

In order to deepen the healing of emotional blockages, it is essential to understand that releasing these internal barriers often requires ongoing, multi-faceted work. In addition to the shamanic practices described above, there are several additional techniques and rituals that can be integrated into the daily routine to promote emotional healing in a more effective and sustained way.

The practice of moon rituals is a powerful shamanic technique for working with the natural cycles of release and renewal. The full moon is an ideal time for release rituals, where you can focus on clearing emotional blockages and accumulated negative energies. During the full moon, the shaman can guide the participant in a release ritual, where they write on a piece of paper all the emotions and traumas that need to be released. Burning this paper in a fire or with a candle can symbolize the release of these energies. On the other hand, the new moon is a time to plant new intentions and start afresh. During the new moon, the shaman can guide the setting of new intentions for emotional healing and personal growth by writing them down and keeping them on the personal altar.

Creating a sacred space remains a fundamental aspect of the healing process. This space should be kept clean and energetically balanced, with the regular burning of sacred herbs for purification. Including elements of nature, such as stones, shells and plants, can help create an atmosphere of serenity and connection. Maintaining a personal altar with healing crystals, candles and spiritual symbols can serve as a focal point for daily spiritual practice.

Self-care rituals are essential to support the emotional healing process. This can include activities that promote joy and satisfaction, such as hobbies, light physical exercise, quality time with loved ones and moments of rest and relaxation. Self-care also involves attention to physical health, with a balanced and adequate diet, hydration and sufficient sleep. Practices such as self-massage with essential oils, relaxing baths and creating a comfortable and welcoming environment at home can make a big difference to overall well-being.

The practice of guided visualizations is a powerful technique for releasing emotional blockages. Visualizations that involve healing scenarios and light can help transform negative energies and promote a state of inner peace. Visualizing a golden or white light entering the body and filling every cell with healing and love can be a powerful daily practice. This visualization can be done during meditation, before bed or in times of need during the day.

Integrating conscious breathing practices is equally important. The regular practice of deep, controlled breathing can help calm the nervous system and promote a sense of relaxation. Techniques such as diaphragmatic breathing or alternate breathing can be performed several times a day to release emotional tension and promote calm. These practices can be integrated into the daily routine, during times of stress or as part of a morning or evening ritual.

Art therapy remains an effective technique for emotional release. Artistic activities, such as drawing, painting or creating mandalas, allow for emotional expression and the release of internal tensions. The creative process can be a form of meditation, where the mind calms down and focuses on the present moment. Creating art inspired by themes of healing and transformation can help channel difficult emotions and find a sense of fulfillment and purpose.

Participating in healing circles or shamanic support groups remains a crucial aspect of the healing process. These groups offer a safe space to share experiences and practices, and to receive support from others who are on the same journey. The exchange of wisdom and healing techniques can offer new insights and strengthen the determination to move forward. The feeling of belonging and connection with others can be a powerful antidote to the sense of isolation that often accompanies emotional blockages.

Gratitude rituals are also key to promoting emotional well-being. Taking a moment throughout the day to reflect on the things you are grateful for can help refocus the mind on positive aspects of life, reducing stress and promoting a sense of contentment. Keeping a gratitude journal, where you write down three things you are grateful for every day, can create a more relaxed and receptive state of mind. This simple act can transform one's outlook on life and promote a deeper sense of peace and harmony.

The practice of yoga and gentle stretching can complement shamanic techniques, helping to release physical and emotional tensions. Specific yoga postures, such as the child's pose and the warrior's pose, promote relaxation and inner strength. Regular yoga practice can help balance the chakras, the body's energy centers, and promote a general sense of well-being. Incorporating breathing and meditation techniques during yoga practice can intensify the healing effects.

Shamanic healing for emotional blockages involves a holistic approach that considers all aspects of the being - physical, emotional, mental and spiritual. By creating an environment conducive to healing, carrying out shamanic journeys, using healing crystals and incorporating meditation and breathing practices, it is possible to treat emotional blockages in an effective and lasting way. These practices not only help relieve the symptoms of emotional blockages, but also promote holistic health, providing a more balanced and harmonious life.

Healing emotional blockages through shamanic practices is an ongoing process that involves integrating various techniques and rituals into daily life. These practices help to release repressed emotions, restore the natural flow of energy and promote balanced emotional health. In addition to the techniques already mentioned, there are other approaches that can be implemented to deepen healing and strengthen emotional well-being.

The use of shamanic drums is a traditional technique that can help release emotional blockages and promote a healing trance state. The rhythmic, repetitive sound of the drum helps induce an altered state of consciousness, allowing the shaman to access spiritual realms and work with subtle energies. The drum can be used during meditations, shamanic journeys or healing rituals to release emotional tensions and promote deep healing. Participants can also use the drum at home, creating their own rhythm for daily meditations or moments of reflection.

The practice of shamanic dances is another powerful technique for emotional release. Dancing allows the body to move in an intuitive and expressive way, helping to release repressed emotions and restore the natural flow of energy. Shamanic dance can be done to the sound of drums, traditional music or even in silence, allowing the participant to connect deeply with their emotions and release them through movement. This practice can be incorporated into the daily routine or performed during specific healing rituals.

Sound therapy with Tibetan bowls and bells is a vibrational practice that can help balance the body's energies and promote emotional release. The sound of Tibetan bowls creates vibrations that resonate with the chakras and help dissolve energy blockages. During a sound therapy session, the shaman or therapist can touch the bowls around the participant's body, allowing the vibrations to penetrate deeply and promote healing. This practice can be carried out regularly as part of a self-care routine.

Forest bathing, or shinrin-yoku, is a practice that involves spending time in nature, especially in forests, to promote healing and well-being. Connecting with nature has a calming and restorative effect, helping to reduce stress and release emotional tension. During a forest bath, the participant is encouraged to walk slowly, observe the details around them and connect with the energy of the trees and plants. This practice can be done regularly to maintain emotional balance and promote connection with nature.

Journaling or therapeutic writing is an effective technique for emotional release. Keeping a journal in which you record thoughts, emotions and daily experiences can help you process feelings and identify patterns that need to be worked on. Therapeutic writing can include specific exercises, such as writing unsent letters to people who have caused emotional pain, or writing down healing intentions and reflections on personal progress. This journal can serve as a tool for self-discovery and self-compassion.

Full and new moon rituals continue to be a powerful practice for emotional release and intention setting. During the full moon, the participant can perform release rituals by writing on a piece of paper the emotions and traumas they wish to release and burning it in a sacred fire. During the new moon, it's a time to plant new intentions for healing and personal growth, writing them down and keeping them on the personal altar. These rituals help to align healing work with natural cycles and promote a sense of renewal and transformation.

Practicing conscious breathing techniques is fundamental to emotional healing. Breathing exercises such as the 4-7-8 breath (inhale for 4 seconds, hold for 7 seconds and exhale slowly for 8 seconds) can help calm the nervous system and promote the release of emotional tensions. Conscious breathing can be integrated into the daily routine, helping to create a foundation of calm and balance.

The practice of protective visualizations can help create a safe and peaceful environment for emotional healing. Before going to sleep, the participant can visualize a protective light around their body and their room, forming a barrier against negative energies. This light can be visualized as a specific color, such as white or gold, which symbolizes protection and peace. Reinforcing this visualization with the repetition of protective mantras, such as "I am safe and protected", can strengthen the feeling of security and promote a more restful sleep.

Integrating mindfulness practices into daily routines remains essential for emotional healing. Mindfulness involves being fully present in the moment, observing thoughts and emotions without judgment. This practice can help break the cycle of rumination and create a space for healthy emotional expression. Daily mindfulness meditations can include observing the breath, listening to the sounds around you or paying full attention to bodily sensations.

Adopting an attitude of self-compassion and patience during the healing process is essential. Recognizing that releasing emotional blockages is a process that requires time and care is fundamental. Treating yourself with kindness and understanding, and celebrating small progress, can relieve pressure and promote a more positive mindset. Regularly practicing self-compassion can help relieve feelings of guilt or shame and promote a sense of self-acceptance and self-love.

Shamanic healing for emotional blockages involves a holistic approach that considers all aspects of the being - physical, emotional, mental and spiritual. By creating an environment conducive to healing, carrying out shamanic journeys, using healing crystals and incorporating meditation and breathing practices, it is possible to treat emotional blockages in an effective and lasting way. These practices not only help relieve the symptoms of emotional blockages, but also promote holistic health, providing a more balanced and harmonious life.

Emotional blockages can manifest in various ways, including difficulty forming deep connections, disproportionate emotional responses and a sense of emotional stagnation. To address these issues effectively, it is essential to integrate ongoing self-care and emotional healing practices into daily life. The shamanic approach offers various techniques and rituals to support this journey.

The practice of creating mandalas is a powerful technique for promoting emotional healing and introspection. Mandalas are symbolic representations of the universe and can be used as tools for meditation and artistic expression. Creating mandalas allows emotions to be expressed non-verbally, helping to release internal tensions and promote a state of balance. The process of drawing or coloring mandalas can be deeply meditative, helping to calm the mind and focus energy on healing.

The use of medicinal plants and herbal teas is another traditional practice in shamanism that can help release emotional blockages. Plants such as chamomile, valerian and passionflower have calming properties and can be used to make teas that help relax the body and mind. Drinking a calming tea before bed can help prepare the body for restful sleep and promote emotional healing during the night. In addition, the preparation and consumption of teas can be incorporated as daily rituals that signal to the body and mind that it is time to relax and release tension.

The practice of journaling or therapeutic writing continues to be a valuable tool for processing and releasing emotions. Writing about experiences, feelings and thoughts can help bring clarity and understanding, allowing emotions to be expressed in a safe and controlled way. Therapeutic writing can include specific exercises, such as writing unsent letters to people who have caused emotional pain, or writing down healing intentions and reflections on personal progress. Keeping a regular journal can serve as a safe space for self-discovery and emotional healing.

Purification rituals are fundamental to maintaining a clean and balanced energetic environment. Burning sacred herbs, such as sage, cedar or palo santo, can help clear accumulated negative energies and prepare the space for healing. These rituals can be performed weekly or as needed, especially after stressful or emotionally intense events. Purification of personal space, such as the home or workplace, can create an environment of peace and serenity, promoting emotional healing.

Practicing guided meditations that involve visualizations of light and healing can help transform negative energies and promote a state of inner peace. Visualizing a golden or white light entering the body and filling every cell with healing and love can be a powerful daily practice. This visualization can be done during meditation, before bed or at times of need during the day. In addition, the use of nature sounds or soothing music during meditations can intensify the healing effects and promote a state of deep relaxation.

Participation in healing circles or shamanic support groups remains a crucial aspect of the healing process. These groups offer a safe space to share experiences and practices, and to receive support from others who are on the same journey. The exchange of wisdom and healing techniques can offer new insights and strengthen the determination to move forward. The feeling of belonging and connection with others can be a powerful antidote to the sense of isolation that often accompanies emotional blockages.

The practice of yoga and gentle stretching can complement shamanic techniques, helping to release physical and emotional tension. Specific yoga postures, such as the child's pose and the warrior's pose, promote relaxation and inner strength. Regular yoga practice can help balance the chakras, the body's energy centers, and promote a general sense of well-being. Incorporating breathing and meditation techniques during yoga practice can intensify the healing effects.

The use of conscious breathing techniques is fundamental to emotional healing. Breathing exercises, such as diaphragmatic breathing or alternate breathing, can help calm the nervous system and promote the release of emotional tensions. Conscious breathing can be integrated into the daily routine, helping to create a foundation of calm and balance. In addition, the practice of conscious breathing can be particularly useful during times of stress or anxiety, helping to restore calm and focus.

Adopting an attitude of self-compassion and patience during the healing process is essential. Recognizing that releasing emotional blockages is a process that requires time and care is fundamental. Treating yourself with kindness and understanding, and celebrating small progress, can relieve pressure and promote a more positive mindset. Regularly practicing self-compassion can help relieve feelings of guilt or shame and promote a sense of self-acceptance and self-love.

Shamanic healing for emotional blockages involves a holistic approach that considers all aspects of the being - physical, emotional, mental and spiritual. By creating an environment conducive to healing, carrying out shamanic journeys, using healing crystals and incorporating meditation and breathing practices, it is possible to treat emotional blockages in an effective and lasting way. These practices not only help to relieve the symptoms of emotional blockages, but also promote holistic health, providing a more balanced and harmonious life.

To ensure the effective release of emotional blockages, it is essential to continue integrating self-care and emotional healing practices that promote sustainable well-being. In addition to the techniques discussed above, there are other complementary approaches that can be implemented to maintain progress and strengthen emotional resilience.

Practicing healing rituals with the help of power animals is an effective shamanic technique for working with emotional blockages. Power animals are guardian spirits that offer guidance, protection and healing. During a shamanic journey, the shaman can find a power animal that resonates with the participant and their emotional needs. This power animal can offer insights and support, helping to release blockages and restore emotional balance. Keeping a representation of the power animal, such as a picture or symbolic object, on the personal altar can strengthen this connection and provide an ongoing sense of protection and guidance.

The practice of gratitude rituals continues to be a powerful technique for promoting emotional healing. Taking a moment every day to reflect on the things you are grateful for helps refocus the mind on positive aspects of life, reducing stress and promoting a sense of contentment. Keeping a gratitude journal, where you write down three things you are grateful for every day, can create a more relaxed and receptive state of mind. This simple act can transform one's outlook on life and promote a deeper sense of peace and harmony.

Sound therapy, using instruments such as Tibetan bowls, gongs and bells, is a vibrational practice that can help balance the body's energies and promote emotional release. The sound of these tools can help dissolve energy blockages and restore the natural flow of energy. During a sound therapy session, the shaman or therapist can play the instruments around the participant's body, allowing the vibrations to penetrate deeply and promote healing. This practice can be carried out regularly as part of a self-care routine.

Ritual baths remain a traditional practice in shamanism that can be used for purification and energy renewal. Preparing a bath with sacred herbs such as lavender, rosemary and chamomile can help relax the body and mind. Adding a few drops of lavender or eucalyptus essential oil can increase the calming effect. During the bath, visualizing the water cleansing all negative energies and bringing a sense of renewal and peace can be a powerful practice. This ritual can be performed weekly or as needed, especially during times of intense stress or sadness.

The practice of protective visualizations can help create a safe and peaceful environment for emotional healing. Before going to sleep, the participant can visualize a protective light around their body and their room, forming a barrier against negative energies. This light can be visualized as a specific color, such as white or gold, which symbolizes protection and peace. Reinforcing this visualization with the repetition of protective mantras, such as "I am safe and protected", can strengthen the feeling of security and promote a more peaceful sleep.

The practice of conscious breathing is fundamental for emotional healing. Breathing exercises, such as 4-7-8 breathing (inhale for 4 seconds, hold for 7 seconds and exhale slowly for 8 seconds), can help calm the nervous system and promote the release of emotional tensions. Conscious breathing can be integrated into the daily routine, helping to create a foundation of calm and balance. In addition, the practice of mindful breathing can be particularly useful during times of stress or anxiety, helping to restore calm and focus.

The practice of mindfulness remains essential for emotional healing. Mindfulness involves being fully present in the moment, observing thoughts and emotions without judgment. This practice can help break the cycle of rumination and create a space for healthy emotional expression. Daily mindfulness meditations can include observing the breath, listening to the sounds around you or paying full attention to bodily sensations.

The integration of art therapy continues to be an effective technique for emotional release. Artistic activities, such as drawing, painting or creating mandalas, allow for emotional expression and the release of internal tensions. The creative process can be a form of meditation, where the mind calms down and focuses on the present moment. Creating art inspired by themes of healing and transformation can help channel difficult emotions and find a sense of fulfillment and purpose.

Participation in healing circles or shamanic support groups remains a crucial aspect of the healing process. These groups offer a safe space to share experiences and practices, and to receive support from others who are on the same journey. The exchange of wisdom and healing techniques can offer new insights and strengthen the determination to move forward. The feeling of belonging and connection with others can be a powerful antidote to the sense of isolation that often accompanies emotional blockages.

Finally, adopting an attitude of self-compassion and patience during the healing process is essential. Recognizing that releasing emotional blockages is a process that requires time and care is fundamental. Treating yourself with kindness and understanding, and celebrating small progress, can relieve pressure and promote a more positive mindset. Regularly practicing self-compassion can help relieve feelings of guilt or shame and promote a sense of self-acceptance and self-love.

Shamanic healing for emotional blockages involves a holistic approach that considers all aspects of the being - physical, emotional, mental and spiritual. By creating an environment conducive to healing, carrying out shamanic journeys, using healing crystals and incorporating meditation and breathing practices, it is possible to treat emotional blockages in an effective and lasting way. These practices not only help to relieve the symptoms of emotional blockages, but also promote holistic health, providing a more balanced and harmonious life.

Chapter 5
Chronic Fatigue

Chronic fatigue is a debilitating condition that affects a person's ability to carry out daily activities efficiently. This condition is not only physical, but can also impact mental and emotional well-being. Understanding the nature of chronic fatigue and its underlying causes is essential to addressing it effectively through shamanic practices.

Chronic fatigue is characterized by a persistent feeling of tiredness that does not improve with rest and can be exacerbated by physical or mental activity. Symptoms can include muscle weakness, joint pain, memory and concentration problems, and a general feeling of malaise. This continuous state of exhaustion can lead to a significant decrease in quality of life, negatively impacting both work performance and social activities.

Identifying the symptoms is the first crucial step in addressing chronic fatigue. People suffering from this condition often report difficulties in completing daily tasks, a constant feeling of exhaustion, and the need for prolonged rest without feeling refreshed. In addition, they may experience sleep disturbances, such as insomnia or non-restorative sleep, which further exacerbates the feeling of tiredness. Identifying these symptoms allows for a more accurate diagnosis and the choice of appropriate healing practices.

The causes of chronic fatigue are varied and can include a combination of physical, emotional and environmental factors. Stress and overload are common causes, where the body and mind are pushed to the limit without sufficient time for recovery. Underlying medical conditions, such as autoimmune diseases or chronic viral infections, can also contribute significantly. In addition, poor diet and sedentary lifestyle habits can exacerbate symptoms, creating a vicious cycle of fatigue and inactivity.

To address chronic fatigue through shamanic practices, it is essential to adopt a holistic approach that considers all aspects of being - physical, emotional, mental and spiritual. Creating an environment conducive to healing is one of the first steps. This environment should be peaceful and free of distractions, allowing for a deep connection with the spiritual world. Purification of the space can be done by burning sacred herbs, such as sage or palo santo, to cleanse any negative energy present.

The next step is to prepare the body and mind for the healing ritual. This can include relaxation techniques such as meditation and deep breathing, which help to calm the nervous system and focus the mind on the healing intention. Visualization practices are also useful, where you can imagine a healing light enveloping the body, restoring vital energy and eliminating exhaustion.

The integration of healing crystals is a common practice in shamanism. Crystals such as rose quartz and amethyst are known for their calming and energizing properties. Placing these crystals at strategic points during meditation or ritual can amplify the healing energy, helping to restore the body's energy balance. In addition, the use of essential oils, such as lavender and eucalyptus, can complement the practice, providing a relaxing and invigorating environment.

The regular practice of shamanic healing techniques can not only relieve the symptoms of chronic fatigue, but also promote holistic health, providing a more balanced and harmonious life. These techniques include keeping a self-care journal, where you can record feelings and progress, helping you to identify patterns and make adjustments as necessary. The shamanic approach is an ongoing journey of self-discovery and healing, where each practice contributes to overall well-being.

The journey to understanding and healing chronic fatigue begins with a deep exploration of the underlying causes. In addition to physical factors, the emotional dimension plays a significant role. Repressed emotions, unresolved traumas and constant stress can drain vital energy, contributing to the persistent feeling of exhaustion. Recognizing and addressing these emotions is crucial to the healing process.

One of the effective techniques for releasing repressed emotions is the shamanic journey. During the journey, the shaman enters an altered state of consciousness, facilitated by the rhythmic sound of drums or rattles, allowing access to spiritual realms where ancestral wisdom resides. On these journeys, the shaman can meet and communicate with spirit guides who offer insights into the emotional causes of chronic fatigue and guidance on how to release these stagnant energies.

The practice of daily meditation is a powerful tool for balancing emotions and restoring energy. Meditations focused on conscious breathing and visualizations of healing light can help calm the mind and recharge the body. Visualizing a golden or white light entering through the top of the head and filling the whole body with vital energy can be especially revitalizing. This practice not only relieves tiredness, but also promotes a sense of peace and well-being.

In addition to meditative practices, the use of medicinal plants is an ancient tradition in shamanism that can be highly beneficial for chronic fatigue. Herbs such as ashwagandha and ginseng are known for their adaptogenic properties, helping the body to adapt to stress and restore energy balance. Drinking teas from these herbs regularly can provide ongoing support for the energy system. The preparation of these teas can be incorporated into daily rituals, creating a routine that signals to the body that it's time to relax and revitalize.

Food also plays a crucial role in managing chronic fatigue. Nutrient-rich foods such as fresh fruit, vegetables, whole grains and lean proteins provide the energy needed for the body to function efficiently. Avoiding processed and sugar-rich foods can prevent energy spikes and dips, maintaining a constant level of vitality throughout the day. In addition, adequate hydration is essential for maintaining energy and cellular function.

Connecting with nature is another fundamental shamanic practice that can help restore vital energy. Spending time outdoors, walking barefoot in the dirt or doing light exercise in a natural environment can have a profoundly revitalizing effect. Nature has an inherent healing energy, and simply interacting with the natural environment can help rebalance the body and mind. This practice, known as earthing, allows the body to absorb the energy of the earth, promoting a sense of well-being and renewal.

Purification rituals are equally important in the treatment of chronic fatigue. Burning sacred herbs such as sage or cedar can cleanse accumulated negative energies, creating a lighter environment conducive to healing. Performing these rituals regularly, especially at times of transition, such as waking up or before going to sleep, can help keep the energy space clean and balanced. In addition, cleansing baths with rock salt and herbs can be a relaxing and invigorating practice, helping to release tension and restore vitality.

Participating in healing circles or support groups can provide a sense of community and emotional support. Sharing experiences and practices with others who are on the same journey can offer new insights and strengthen the determination to move forward. The feeling of belonging and being understood can be a powerful antidote to emotional and mental exhaustion.

The shamanic approach to healing chronic fatigue is an ongoing process that integrates spiritual, emotional and physical practices. By adopting a routine that includes meditation, the use of medicinal plants, healthy eating, connecting with nature and purification rituals, it is possible to restore vital energy and live a more balanced and harmonious life.

To further understand and treat chronic fatigue, it is essential to explore the connection between the mind and the body. Chronic fatigue often results from a cycle of negative thoughts and stressful emotions that deplete vital energy.

Breaking this cycle requires an approach that incorporates self-care practices and emotional healing techniques.

The practice of mindfulness is a powerful tool for breaking the cycle of negative thoughts. Mindfulness involves paying full attention to the present moment, observing thoughts and sensations without judgment. Devoting a few minutes a day to mindfulness meditation can help calm the mind and reduce stress. During meditation, focusing on the breath and allowing thoughts to pass without getting caught up in them can create a state of inner peace, which is essential for restoring energy.

Another effective technique is practicing gratitude. Keeping a gratitude journal, where you write down three things you are grateful for every day, can refocus your mind on positive aspects of life. This simple practice can transform one's mental outlook, reducing stress and promoting a sense of well-being. Gratitude helps release feel-good hormones such as serotonin, which contribute to a greater sense of energy and vitality.

Integrating conscious breathing practices is fundamental to managing chronic fatigue. Techniques such as diaphragmatic breathing, where you breathe deeply through the nose, expanding the abdomen, and exhale slowly through the mouth, can help calm the nervous system and recharge energy. Performing breathing exercises several times a day, especially during times of stress, can promote a state of deep relaxation and renew vitality.

Shamanic healing also involves using spiritual connection rituals to restore energy. Full and new moon rituals are powerful times to work on the energy of renewal and release. During the full moon, performing a release ritual, where you write on a piece of paper the energies and emotions that need to be released, and then burn the paper, can symbolize the release of these charges. On the new moon, setting clear intentions for the next cycle and symbolically planting them on an altar or in a garden can help cultivate renewed energy.

Shamanic instruments, such as drums and rattles, are valuable tools for altering states of consciousness and promoting healing. The rhythmic sound of the drum can induce a deep meditative state, facilitating the spiritual journey. During these journeys, the shaman can meet spirit guides who offer insights and guidance on how to restore vital energy. Integrating regular shamanic drumming sessions can help maintain energy balance and promote ongoing healing.

Sound therapy is another effective practice for treating chronic fatigue. Specific sounds, such as binaural frequencies and relaxing music, can help balance brain waves and promote a state of deep relaxation. Listening to these frequencies during meditation or before bed can help calm the mind and restore energy. Creating a relaxing sound environment with soft music and nature sounds can transform the healing space, making it more conducive to rest and revitalization.

Connecting with power animals is a shamanic practice that can offer strength and guidance. Each power animal has unique characteristics and wisdom that can be invoked to support the healing journey. For example, the bear is often associated with strength and introspection, while the eagle symbolizes vision and freedom. Meditating on the power animal and invoking its qualities during times of fatigue can provide a sense of support and renewal.

Light physical exercise is crucial for maintaining energy and vitality. Activities such as walking, yoga or tai chi not only help to strengthen the body, but also promote the circulation of vital energy. Regular exercise can help release endorphins, the feel-good hormones that combat feelings of fatigue. It is important to choose activities that are enjoyable and that respect the body's limits, avoiding overload.

The importance of proper nutrition cannot be underestimated. A diet rich in whole foods, fresh vegetables, fruit, lean proteins and healthy fats provides the nutrients needed to maintain energy. Vitamin and mineral supplements, such as vitamin D, B-complex and magnesium, can also be beneficial in combating chronic fatigue. Avoiding processed foods, refined sugar and excessive caffeine can prevent energy peaks followed by sudden drops, maintaining a constant level of vitality.

Continuing to explore shamanic practices to treat chronic fatigue, the importance of energy balance is a key aspect. Chronic fatigue often results from energetic imbalances that can be restored through specific energetic and spiritual healing practices.

The laying on of hands technique, also known as energy healing, is a traditional practice in shamanism that can help restore energetic balance. The shaman or practitioner places their hands on or near the patient's body, channeling healing energy to specific areas where energy is blocked or depleted. This technique can be especially effective for relieving muscle tension and promoting a feeling of deep relaxation. During the session, the patient may feel warmth, tingling or other sensations as the energy flows, helping to restore balance and vitality.

The practice of grounding is another important technique for restoring energy. Grounding involves connecting directly with the earth, whether by walking barefoot on the grass, sitting on the ground or meditating outdoors. This direct connection with the earth helps to release excess static energy and absorb the vital energy of nature. Regular grounding can promote a sense of stability and renewal, helping to combat chronic fatigue.

The use of purification baths is a shamanic practice that can be integrated into a daily or weekly routine. Herbal baths with rock salt, lavender, rosemary or eucalyptus can help cleanse the negative energies accumulated in the body and revitalize energy. Adding healing crystals such as amethyst or rose quartz to the bath water can amplify the healing effects. These baths should be taken in a quiet environment, with soft lighting and relaxing music, to create a deeply restorative experience.

Crystal therapy is a complementary practice that can be used to balance the chakras and restore vital energy. Each crystal has specific properties that can help balance different aspects of the body's energy. For example, amethyst is known for its calming and protective properties, while citrine is used to increase energy and vitality. Placing crystals at strategic points on the body or around the healing space can help harmonize energy and promote a state of balance.

Gentle physical exercise, such as yoga or tai chi, is also essential for maintaining energy and vitality. These exercises not only strengthen the body, but also promote the circulation of vital energy, known as "chi" or "prana". Specific yoga postures, such as the child's pose or the warrior's pose, can help release accumulated tension and revitalize the body. Practicing these exercises in a natural environment can increase the benefits, allowing the body to absorb the healing energy of nature.

Food plays a crucial role in maintaining energy. A balanced diet, rich in whole foods, fresh vegetables, fruit, lean proteins and healthy fats, provides the nutrients needed for the body to function efficiently. Avoiding processed and sugar-rich foods can prevent energy peaks and dips, maintaining a constant level of vitality. Drinking plenty of water and avoiding dehydration is also essential for maintaining energy throughout the day.

Practicing daily rituals of gratitude and intention can help refocus the mind and energy on positive aspects of life. Starting and ending the day with a moment of reflection and gratitude can create a mental state of contentment and peace. Keeping a gratitude journal, where you write down the things you are grateful for on a daily basis, can help focus your mind on the positive and promote a sense of well-being.

Release rituals, especially during the full moon, are powerful moments to release energies and emotions that no longer serve you. Writing down on paper the feelings, thoughts and energies that need to be released and then burning the paper in a fire or with a candle can symbolize the release of these charges. This ritual helps create space for new energies and intentions, promoting renewal and vitality.

The shamanic approach to healing chronic fatigue is an ongoing journey that integrates spiritual, emotional and physical practices. By adopting a routine that includes laying on of hands techniques, grounding, purification baths, crystal therapy, gentle physical exercise, a balanced diet and daily rituals, it is possible to restore vital energy and live a more balanced and harmonious life. Each practice contributes to overall well-being, offering a path to renewal and lasting vitality.

To complete the shamanic approach to treating chronic fatigue, it is essential to integrate practices that promote lasting balance and that can be maintained over the long term. The continuity of these practices is fundamental to ensuring that vital energy is constantly renewed and that physical, mental and spiritual well-being is sustained.

One of the central practices is keeping a self-care diary. This diary should include daily records of the practices carried out, energy levels, emotions and thoughts. Writing down progress, challenges and reflections helps to monitor the effectiveness of healing practices and identify patterns. This continuous record allows for necessary adjustments to self-care routines and provides a clear vision of the healing journey.

The practice of visualization and meditation techniques should be an integral part of the daily routine. Visualizing a constant flow of healing energy entering the body and radiating light and vitality throughout the being can help to keep the energy renewed. This practice can be done in the morning to start the day with energy and in the evening to release accumulated tension. Guided meditations that focus on healing and revitalization can also be used to promote a state of inner peace and renewal.

Periodic purification rituals are crucial for keeping the energy space clean. In addition to purification baths and the burning of sacred herbs, energetic cleansing of the living environment should be carried out regularly. This can include using essential oils in diffusers, placing healing crystals at strategic points in the house and practicing smoking in every room. Keeping the environment free of stagnant energies helps to create a space conducive to rest and recovery.

Continuous connection with nature should be a priority. Spending time outdoors, hiking in natural environments and meditating in green spaces can have a profoundly revitalizing effect. Nature offers a constant source of healing energy that can be absorbed by the body. Activities such as gardening, where you work directly with the earth, can also promote a sense of connection and energetic renewal.

Lunar cycles offer unique opportunities to work with the energy of renewal and release. Performing rituals during the full moon to release energies and emotions that no longer serve, and during the new moon to set new intentions and goals, can help maintain energetic balance. These rituals should be accompanied by meditations and visualizations specific to each lunar phase, making the most of the energies available.

The integration of conscious breathing practices is fundamental to maintaining calm and energy throughout the day. Techniques such as diaphragmatic breathing and the 4-7-8 technique can be used regularly to reduce stress and promote mental clarity. Performing these practices during moments of transition, such as waking up, before meals and before bed, can help maintain a constant state of relaxation and vitality.

The practice of gratitude and intention rituals should be maintained to cultivate a positive mindset. Starting and ending the day with moments of reflection on the things you are grateful for can help create a mental state of contentment and peace. Keeping a gratitude journal can reinforce this practice, helping to focus the mind on positive aspects of life and promoting a continuous sense of well-being.

Sound therapy, including the use of shamanic drums and relaxing music, should be integrated into the self-care routine. The rhythmic sound of the drum can be used to induce deep meditative states, facilitating healing and energy renewal. Listening to relaxing music and nature sounds, especially during meditation and before bed, can help calm the mind and promote restful sleep.

Finally, it is essential to cultivate an attitude of self-compassion and acceptance throughout the healing journey. Recognizing that chronic fatigue is a complex condition that requires time and patience to treat is key to maintaining motivation and resilience. Treating yourself with kindness, celebrating small progress and being patient with yourself during challenging times can promote a positive and sustaining mindset.

The shamanic approach to healing chronic fatigue is a continuous path that integrates spiritual, emotional and physical practices. By adopting a routine that includes visualization techniques, meditation, purification rituals, connecting with nature, conscious breathing practices and gratitude rituals, it is possible to maintain vital energy and live a balanced and harmonious life. This holistic approach not only relieves the symptoms of chronic fatigue, but also promotes general well-being, offering a path to renewal and lasting vitality.

Chapter 6
Chronic Pain

Chronic pain is a debilitating condition that affects many people's quality of life. Unlike acute pain, which is temporary and usually the result of an injury or inflammation, chronic pain persists for long periods, often without a clear cause or complete resolution. The shamanic approach offers holistic methods for identifying, understanding and treating chronic pain, promoting relief and lasting well-being.

Identifying the problem is the first step in treating chronic pain. This type of pain can arise from a variety of conditions, including diseases such as arthritis, fibromyalgia, old injuries, or even back problems. It is important to understand the nature of the pain, its location and intensity, and how it affects the individual's daily life. Chronic pain not only impacts physical well-being, but can also lead to emotional problems such as anxiety and depression, creating a vicious cycle of suffering.

The symptoms of chronic pain vary widely. They can include constant or intermittent pain, a burning sensation, throbbing pain, stiffness and tenderness in the affected areas. In addition, chronic pain can cause fatigue, insomnia, and difficulty in carrying out daily activities. These symptoms can lead to social isolation, loss of productivity and a general decrease in quality of life. Recognizing these symptoms is crucial to developing an effective healing strategy.

The common causes of chronic pain are varied. Injuries and illnesses are frequent causes; for example, an old sports injury that has never completely healed or diseases such as arthritis that cause ongoing inflammation in the joints. A sedentary lifestyle is also a significant cause, as lack of movement can lead to muscle stiffness and pain. In addition, emotional factors such as stress and trauma can contribute to the manifestation and perpetuation of chronic pain, since the body and mind are intrinsically connected.

Preparing for a shamanic healing ritual begins with creating a sacred space. This space should be quiet, free of distractions and energetically clean. The space can be purified by burning sacred herbs such as sage or cedar, which help to eliminate negative energies and prepare the environment for healing. Creating an altar with meaningful items such as healing crystals, candles and plants can help focus the intention of the ritual and create an atmosphere conducive to healing.

The materials needed for the ritual can include drums or rattles to facilitate entering trance states, specific healing crystals to relieve pain, such as amethyst and clear quartz, and essential oils of lavender or eucalyptus, which have anti-inflammatory and analgesic properties. The shaman can also use personal objects of the individual being treated to strengthen the energetic and spiritual connection during the ritual.

The shamanic journey is a powerful technique used to treat chronic pain. During the journey, the shaman enters an altered state of consciousness, usually induced by the rhythmic sound of the drum or rattle. This state allows the shaman to access the spiritual realms in search of guidance and healing. The journey can reveal the underlying causes of chronic pain, which is often related to energetic imbalances or past traumas.

At the beginning of the journey, the shaman focuses on the intention of healing, invoking the guiding spirits and the elements of nature to assist in the process. Deep, rhythmic breathing helps to stabilize the body and mind, facilitating the transition to the altered state of consciousness. During the journey, the shaman may meet and interact with power animals or ancestral spirits, who offer wisdom and insights into the origin of pain and the most appropriate healing methods.

A common practice during the journey is the visualization of healing lights. The shaman visualizes a bright, healing light entering the individual's body, focusing on the areas affected by the pain. This light can be of various colors, each with its own specific healing properties. For example, green light is often associated with physical healing, while blue light can bring calm and pain relief. The shaman directs this light to the areas of pain, promoting the release of energy blockages and restoring the flow of vital energy.

Extracting negative energies is another technique used during the journey. The shaman identifies and removes any negative energies or entities that may be contributing to chronic pain. This practice may involve the use of crystals, feathers or other sacred objects to extract and transmute these energies, restoring balance to the body and spirit. After the extraction, the shaman can fill the empty space with positive and healing energy, reinforcing the healing process.

Chants and mantras are essential tools in the shamanic journey. Sound has a vibrational frequency that can help realign the body's energy and promote healing. The shaman uses traditional chants, passed down from generation to generation, known for their healing properties. These chants create a resonance that helps dissolve energy blockages and relieve pain. In addition, the use of repetitive mantras can help focus the mind and intensify the healing intention.

After the journey, it is crucial to have a period of integration, where the shaman and the individual being treated reflect on the experiences and insights gained. This reflection helps to consolidate the energetic changes and apply the lessons learned to everyday life. The shaman can offer additional guidance on daily practices that can support the continuity of the healing process, such as meditation, breathing exercises and the use of medicinal herbs.

The regular practice of relaxation techniques is fundamental to the management of chronic pain. Meditation, yoga and stretching exercises can help relieve muscle tension and reduce the perception of pain. Conscious breathing, where you inhale deeply through your nose and exhale slowly through your mouth, can be particularly effective in calming the nervous system and promoting relaxation. These practices not only help manage pain, but also improve overall quality of life.

Shamanic healing of chronic pain is a holistic process that integrates body, mind and spirit. By addressing the underlying causes of pain and promoting energetic healing, it is possible to find relief and restore balance. The combination of shamanic journeying, negative energy extraction techniques and daily relaxation practices provides a comprehensive approach to the treatment of chronic pain, offering hope and relief to those suffering from this debilitating condition.

In addition to journeying and extraction techniques, shamanism offers other therapeutic practices that can be incorporated into the treatment of chronic pain. The use of medicinal plants is one such practice, which combines ancestral wisdom with natural therapeutic benefits. Certain plants have analgesic and anti-inflammatory properties that can help relieve pain and promote healing.

Herbs such as arnica, ginger and turmeric are widely used in shamanic medicine to treat chronic pain. Arnica, for example, is known for its anti-inflammatory properties and can be applied topically to reduce pain and swelling. Ginger, on the other hand, has compounds that block the production of chemicals that cause inflammation in the body. Turmeric, rich in curcumin, is also a potent natural anti-inflammatory. These plants can be consumed as teas, infusions or applied as compresses to painful areas.

Heat and cold therapy is another technique used to relieve chronic pain. Applying heat to the affected areas can help relax tense muscles and increase blood flow, promoting healing. The use of hot water bags or warm compresses is effective for this purpose. On the other hand, applying cold can help reduce inflammation and swelling. Cold compresses or ice packs can be used to relieve acute pain and control inflammation. Alternating between heat and cold can provide significant relief and promote recovery.

Massage therapy is a common practice in shamanic healing. Through massage techniques, it is possible to release tension built up in the muscles and improve blood circulation. The shaman's therapeutic touch, combined with the use of essential oils such as lavender oil, which has relaxing properties, can help relieve pain and promote a state of deep relaxation. Massage can be adapted to the specific needs of each individual, focusing on the areas that most need relief.

Acupressure, a technique that involves applying pressure to specific points on the body, can also be effective in treating chronic pain. This practice is based on traditional Chinese medicine and is used to release energy blockages and restore the flow of vital energy. The acupressure points are stimulated with the fingers, promoting pain relief and energy balance. This technique can be combined with other shamanic practices to enhance the healing effects.

Sound therapy, using drums, Tibetan bells and other percussion instruments, is another therapeutic approach to treating chronic pain. Sound has a vibrational frequency that can help realign the body's energy and promote healing. The shaman uses specific rhythms to induce states of relaxation and meditation, helping to relieve pain and restore balance. Sound therapy can be carried out during healing sessions or as part of a daily wellness practice.

Connecting with nature is a fundamental aspect of shamanic practice and can have a profound impact on chronic pain management. Spending time outdoors, whether walking in forests, sitting by a river or gardening, can help reduce stress and promote healing. Nature has a calming and revitalizing effect, and regular interaction with the natural environment can improve physical and emotional well-being. The shaman can guide the individual to perform rituals of gratitude and offerings to the earth, strengthening the connection with the natural elements and promoting harmony.

In addition to physical and energetic practices, the shamanic approach to healing chronic pain also involves transforming limiting beliefs and negative thought patterns. Chronic pain can be exacerbated by a pessimistic mindset or feelings of hopelessness. The shaman works with the individual to identify and transform these patterns, promoting a positive and empowered mindset. The practice of daily affirmations and positive visualizations can help reprogram the mind to focus on healing and well-being.

Shamanic healing of chronic pain is a continuous and integrated process involving body, mind and spirit. By combining traditional therapeutic practices with modern wellness approaches, it is possible to find relief and promote a better quality of life. Through the use of medicinal plants, heat and cold therapies, massage, acupressure, sound therapy and the connection with nature, the shaman offers a comprehensive and holistic approach to the treatment of chronic pain, helping individuals to find balance and lasting relief.

The integration of spiritual practices is a vital component in the shamanic approach to treating chronic pain. Spiritual healing involves connecting deeply with the inner self, spirit guides and the elements of nature. This connection can provide significant pain relief and promote a sense of well-being and balance.

One of the most powerful spiritual practices is guided meditation. During meditation, the individual is guided to visualize healing energy entering the body. This energy can be visualized as a bright light that permeates every cell, removing blockages and restoring the flow of vital energy. Guided meditation helps to calm the mind and focus the healing intention, promoting a state of deep relaxation and pain relief.

The practice of gratitude is another important aspect of spiritual healing. Setting aside time each day to reflect on the things you are grateful for can transform your perception of pain and promote a positive mindset. Keeping a gratitude journal, where you record three things you are grateful for every day, can help refocus your mind on positive aspects of life, lessening the impact of chronic pain. Gratitude creates a resonance of positive energy that can improve general well-being.

Purification rituals are essential for spiritual healing. Smoking with sacred herbs such as sage, cedar or palo santo helps to cleanse negative energies and prepare the environment for healing. The smoke from these herbs is considered an offering to the spirits, establishing a connection between the physical and spiritual worlds. Performing these rituals regularly can help maintain energy balance and promote spiritual health.

Creating a personal altar is a spiritual practice that can support the healing process. This altar can include items that symbolize the healing intention, such as crystals, candles, plants and meaningful personal objects. The altar serves as a focal point for meditation and daily rituals, helping to focus energy and intention. Keeping the altar clean and energetically balanced is crucial to the success of spiritual practices.

Music and sound play a crucial role in spiritual healing. Chants, mantras and percussion instruments such as Tibetan drums and bells have the power to alter states of consciousness and promote healing. Sound creates a vibrational frequency that can help dissolve energy blockages and relieve pain. The practice of chanting or listening to recordings of shamanic music can be incorporated into the daily routine to promote spiritual well-being.

Working with crystals is a common practice in shamanic healing. Each crystal has a unique vibrational frequency that can be used to balance the body's energy. Crystals such as amethyst, clear quartz and rose quartz are particularly effective in relieving pain and promoting healing. These crystals can be placed on affected areas of the body, carried in the pocket or worn as jewelry. The regular practice of meditation with crystals can intensify the healing effects.

Practicing protective visualizations can help create a safe and peaceful environment, which is essential for the healing process. Before going to sleep or during moments of meditation, the individual can visualize a protective light around their body, forming a barrier against negative energies. This light can be visualized as a specific color, such as white or gold, which symbolizes protection and peace. Reinforcing this visualization with the repetition of protective mantras can strengthen the feeling of security and promote more restful sleep.

The importance of community and social support cannot be underestimated in healing chronic pain. Participating in healing circles or support groups can provide a sense of belonging and emotional support. Sharing experiences and practices with others who are on the same journey can offer new insights and strengthen the resolve to move forward. Community offers a safe space for expression and healing, fostering a sense of connection and mutual support.

Transforming limiting beliefs and negative thought patterns is essential for spiritual healing. Chronic pain can be exacerbated by a pessimistic mindset or feelings of hopelessness. The shaman works with the individual to identify and transform these patterns, promoting a positive and empowered mindset. The practice of daily affirmations and positive visualizations can help reprogram the mind to focus on healing and well-being.

The spiritual healing of chronic pain is a holistic process that involves body, mind and spirit. By integrating spiritual practices such as meditation, gratitude, purification rituals, crystal work and community participation, it is possible to find relief and promote a better quality of life. The combination of these practices offers a comprehensive and holistic approach to the treatment of chronic pain, helping individuals to find balance and lasting relief.

Healing chronic pain through shamanism is not only a reactive approach, but also a preventative one. It is essential to incorporate daily practices that support energetic balance and prevent pain from returning. These practices help to strengthen the body and mind, promoting a continuous state of well-being.

The daily practice of mindfulness is a powerful tool for managing chronic pain. Mindfulness involves being present in the moment, observing thoughts and sensations without judgment. This practice can be carried out through short meditations throughout the day or simply by taking a few minutes to breathe deeply and reconnect with the present. Mindfulness helps to reduce emotional reactivity and create a space of inner calm, reducing the perception of pain.

Maintaining a light exercise routine is essential for general health and pain management. Activities such as walking, yoga and tai chi not only help reduce muscle pain and stiffness, but also promote the release of endorphins, which are the body's natural painkillers. Regular movement improves blood circulation, increases flexibility and strengthens muscles, helping to reduce chronic pain.

A balanced diet plays a crucial role in the prevention and management of chronic pain. A diet rich in nutrients, natural anti-inflammatories, and low in refined sugars and processed foods can help reduce inflammation and pain. Foods such as fruits, vegetables, nuts, seeds, fish rich in omega-3 and spices such as turmeric and ginger are known for their anti-inflammatory properties. Staying hydrated is also essential for the healthy functioning of the body and the reduction of pain.

Practicing gratitude rituals when waking up and before going to sleep can positively influence the perception of pain. Starting and ending the day with a moment of gratitude helps to set a positive tone and cultivate a mindset of abundance. This ritual can include giving thanks for your body, your health, small daily victories and any other positive aspect of life. Keeping a gratitude journal where you record these thoughts can serve as a constant reminder of the positive, reducing the stress and anxiety that can aggravate pain.

Creating a sacred space in the home, where rituals and meditations can be performed regularly, supports the maintenance of inner peace and energy balance. This space can include an altar with crystals, candles, plants and other meaningful objects. Keeping this space clean and energetically balanced with the regular burning of sacred herbs such as sage or palo santo is crucial for the continuity of spiritual practices.

Practicing conscious breathing techniques throughout the day can help reduce tension and anxiety, preparing the body for a state of deep relaxation. Simple breathing exercises, such as inhaling deeply through the nose and exhaling slowly through the mouth, can be done at any time to calm the nervous system. The 4-7-8 breathing technique is particularly effective for inducing relaxation and can be practiced during times of stress or as part of a morning or evening ritual.

The use of positive visualizations during the day can also influence the perception of pain. Visualizing peaceful and pleasant scenarios, such as a walk in a forest or a day at the beach, can help reduce stress and anxiety, preparing the mind for a state of well-being. These visualizations can be integrated into meditation practice or done while lying in bed, waiting to fall asleep.

The importance of self-compassion and patience with oneself when dealing with chronic pain cannot be underestimated. Recognizing that the journey to improving quality of life can take time and that every step, no matter how small, is progress towards well-being. Treating yourself with kindness and understanding, celebrating small victories and being patient with yourself are essential components of healing.

Connecting with the community and social support are fundamental in managing chronic pain. Participating in healing circles or support groups can provide a sense of belonging and emotional support. Sharing experiences and practices with others who are on the same journey can offer new insights and strengthen the resolve to move forward. Community offers a safe space for expression and healing, fostering a sense of connection and mutual support.

Healing chronic pain through shamanism is an ongoing process that involves integrating various holistic practices into daily life. By creating an environment conducive to healing, practicing mindfulness, maintaining a balanced diet, performing light physical exercise and participating in community, it is possible to find relief and promote a better quality of life. These practices not only help to reduce pain, but also promote general well-being, providing a more balanced and harmonious life.

Chapter 7
Digestive Problems

Digestive problems are common conditions that can affect people of all ages. These conditions include a wide range of symptoms, such as abdominal pain, bloating, gas, constipation, diarrhea, heartburn and indigestion. Digestion is a complex process involving several parts of the body, including the stomach, intestines, liver, pancreas and gallbladder. Any dysfunction in one of these areas can result in digestive problems.

Identifying the symptoms of digestive problems is crucial for effective treatment. Abdominal pain can range from mild discomfort to severe pain, depending on the underlying cause. Bloating is often described as a feeling of fullness or pressure in the abdomen. Gas can cause discomfort and pain, and may be accompanied by excessive eructations or flatulence. Constipation is characterized by infrequent or difficult bowel movements, while diarrhea involves frequent, watery bowel movements. Heartburn is a burning sensation in the chest, usually caused by acid reflux, and indigestion can include a feeling of discomfort or burning in the stomach after eating.

In addition to the physical symptoms, digestive problems can significantly impact a person's mental and emotional health. Chronic pain and discomfort can lead to stress, anxiety and depression. This creates a vicious cycle, where stress and anxiety can, in turn, exacerbate digestive problems.

The shamanic approach to treating digestive problems involves understanding not only the physical symptoms, but also the underlying causes and the emotional and spiritual aspects that can contribute to these conditions. In shamanism, it is believed that the body, mind and spirit are interconnected, and that imbalances in any of these areas can manifest as physical illnesses.

Digestive problems can have various causes, including poor diet, stress and anxiety, infections, the use of certain medications, and medical conditions such as irritable bowel syndrome (IBS), inflammatory bowel disease (IBD) and celiac disease. Identifying the specific cause is the first step in developing an effective treatment plan.

Poor diet is a common cause of digestive problems. Diets rich in processed foods, saturated fats, refined sugars and low in fiber can lead to digestive disorders. In addition, eating too quickly, not chewing food properly and eating at irregular times can also contribute to digestive problems. A balanced diet, rich in fiber, fruit, vegetables and water, can help promote digestive health.

Stress and anxiety are significant factors that can aggravate digestive problems. The digestive system is highly sensitive to emotions, and stress can cause or exacerbate symptoms such as abdominal pain, bloating, constipation and diarrhea. Stress management techniques such as meditation, deep breathing and yoga can be useful for relieving these symptoms.

Bacterial and viral infections can also cause digestive problems. Helicobacter pylori infection, for example, is a common cause of gastric ulcers and gastritis. Other infections, such as viral gastroenteritis, can cause diarrhea and vomiting. Treatment for these infections usually involves the use of antibiotics or antiviral drugs, as well as supportive care such as hydration and rest.

The use of certain medications, such as non-steroidal anti-inflammatory drugs (NSAIDs), antibiotics and blood pressure medications, can cause digestive side effects. These drugs can irritate the stomach lining, alter the intestinal flora or affect bowel movements. It's important to discuss any digestive symptoms with a healthcare professional to adjust medication as necessary.

Finally, underlying medical conditions such as irritable bowel syndrome (IBS), inflammatory bowel disease (IBD) and celiac disease can cause chronic digestive problems. These conditions require a proper diagnosis and an individualized treatment plan to control symptoms and improve quality of life.

The shamanic approach to treating digestive problems combines traditional healing practices with a holistic understanding of the individual. This includes purification rituals, the use of medicinal plants, meditation, and relaxation techniques to restore balance and promote healing. Integrating these practices can help relieve digestive symptoms, improve general health and promote a sense of well-being.

Purification is a central practice in shamanism, especially when it comes to digestive problems. Purification rituals help to cleanse negative energies and prepare the body and spirit for healing. These rituals can include smoking with sacred herbs, herbal baths and the creation of sacred spaces.

Smoking is a technique widely used to purify the environment and the body. Herbs such as sage, rosemary and fennel are burned to generate a smoke that cleanses negative energies. During smoking, it is important to maintain a clear intention of healing and purification. Passing the smoke around the body, especially in the abdominal area, can help relieve digestive discomfort. In addition, smoking the environment where you spend most of your time can create a more harmonious and healing space.

Herbal baths are another effective practice for purifying and relieving digestive problems. Herbs such as chamomile, peppermint and ginger have calming and anti-inflammatory properties that can help relieve pain and inflammation in the digestive system. Preparing a bath with these herbs and immersing yourself in it can help relax the body and mind, promoting a feeling of general well-being. In addition, these baths can be combined with meditation and deep breathing to enhance their healing effects.

The creation of a sacred space is fundamental to any shamanic healing practice. This space should be quiet and free of distractions, allowing for a deep connection with the spiritual world. You can create an altar with elements from nature, such as stones, shells and plants, which symbolize the healing intention. Keeping this space clean and energetically balanced, performing purification rituals regularly, is essential to maintaining an environment conducive to healing.

The use of medicinal plants is an integral part of the shamanic approach to treating digestive problems. Plants have healing properties that can help relieve symptoms and treat the underlying causes of digestive problems. Here are some commonly used plants:

Chamomile: Known for its calming properties, chamomile can help relieve inflammation and pain in the digestive system. Drinking chamomile tea regularly can help reduce bloating and improve digestion.

Peppermint: Peppermint is effective in relieving symptoms such as abdominal pain, bloating and gas. Peppermint essential oil can be used topically on the abdominal area or inhaled to relieve symptoms.

Ginger: Ginger has anti-inflammatory properties and is particularly useful for treating nausea and indigestion. It can be consumed in the form of tea, capsules or added to food.

Aloe Vera: Known for its healing properties, aloe vera can help relieve inflammation and irritation in the digestive tract. Drinking aloe vera juice can help promote healing and improve digestion.

Fennel: Fennel is effective in relieving gas and cramps. Drinking fennel tea after meals can help improve digestion and relieve abdominal discomfort.

In addition to the use of medicinal plants, meditation and relaxation techniques are important components of shamanic treatment for digestive problems. Meditation helps to calm the mind and body, reducing stress and anxiety that can exacerbate digestive symptoms. Practicing meditation regularly can help promote a state of balance and well-being.

Deep breathing techniques are also effective for relieving digestive discomfort. Breathing deeply through the nose, expanding the abdomen, and exhaling slowly through the mouth can help relax the abdominal muscles and promote blood circulation in the area. This practice can be done several times a day, especially during times of stress or discomfort.

The integration of these cleansing practices, the use of medicinal plants, meditation and relaxation techniques can help relieve digestive symptoms and promote improved general health. Shamanism offers a holistic approach that considers the individual as a whole, treating not only the physical symptoms, but also the emotional and spiritual aspects that can contribute to digestive problems.

Meditation is an essential practice in the shamanic treatment of digestive problems. It helps to calm the mind, reduce stress and create a state of deep relaxation, which is crucial for the proper functioning of the digestive system. Regular meditation practice can significantly improve digestive health, relieving symptoms such as abdominal pain, bloating and indigestion.

There are various meditation techniques that can be used to promote digestive health. One of the most effective is guided meditation. This technique involves following the instructions of a guide who leads the mind through a series of relaxing images and thoughts. During guided meditation, the practitioner is encouraged to visualize a peaceful place, such as a forest or a beach, where they feel safe and at peace. This visualization helps to reduce tension and promote a state of calm, which can relieve digestive discomfort.

Another effective technique is breath-focused meditation. This practice involves concentrating on your breathing, observing each inhale and exhale. Deep, conscious breathing helps to relax the abdominal muscles and improve blood circulation in the digestive area. To practice this technique, sit comfortably, close your eyes and breathe deeply through your nose, expanding your abdomen. Hold your breath for a few seconds and then exhale slowly through your mouth. Repeat this process several times, allowing each breath to bring a feeling of relaxation and well-being.

Mindfulness meditation is another practice that can benefit digestive health. Mindfulness involves paying attention to the present moment, observing thoughts and sensations without judgment. This practice helps to reduce stress and anxiety, which can exacerbate digestive problems. To practice mindfulness, find a quiet place, sit comfortably and focus on the sensations in your body. Notice any tension or discomfort in the abdominal area and allow these sensations to gradually dissipate. Concentrate on your breathing and allow your mind to calm down.

In addition to meditation, relaxation techniques are fundamental for digestive health. Progressive relaxation is a technique that involves tensing and relaxing different muscle groups in the body. This practice helps to release the tension built up in the muscles, promoting a state of deep relaxation. To practice progressive relaxation, lie down comfortably and start tensing and relaxing the muscles in your feet, gradually moving up your body until you reach your head. Concentrate on the feeling of relaxation that follows the release of tension.

Yoga is another relaxation practice that can improve digestive health. Certain yoga poses are especially effective for relieving digestive symptoms and promoting healthy digestion. Child's pose, for example, helps to relax the abdominal muscles and reduce bloating. To practice this pose, kneel on the floor, sit on your heels and lean forward, extending your arms in front of you and resting your forehead on the floor. Hold this position for a few minutes, breathing deeply and allowing your body to relax.

Another effective posture is the spinal twist. This posture helps to stimulate digestion and relieve constipation. To practice the spinal twist, sit on the floor with your legs stretched out in front of you. Bend your right knee and place your right foot on the floor next to your left knee. Turn your torso to the right, placing your left hand on your right knee and your right hand on the floor behind you. Hold this position for a few minutes, breathing deeply and allowing the twist to massage the digestive organs.

The regular practice of yoga and meditation can help create a state of balance and harmony in the body, promoting digestive health and relieving symptoms of abdominal discomfort. In addition to these practices, it is important to maintain a healthy and balanced diet, rich in fiber, fruits and vegetables, and to avoid processed and fatty foods that can aggravate digestive problems.

The shamanic approach to treating digestive problems combines these meditation and relaxation practices with a holistic understanding of the individual. By treating the body, mind and spirit as an interconnected unit, shamanism offers a comprehensive approach to healing and well-being. Integrating these practices into the daily routine can help relieve digestive symptoms, improve general health and promote a sense of peace and balance.

Breathing practices are fundamental to digestive health, as they help regulate the nervous system and promote relaxation. Conscious breathing can relieve symptoms such as abdominal pain, bloating and indigestion. In addition, connecting with nature is an integral part of shamanism, providing a healing and balancing environment that can significantly benefit the digestive system.

One effective breathing technique is diaphragmatic breathing, also known as abdominal breathing. This practice involves breathing deeply through the nose, allowing the abdomen to expand, and then exhaling slowly through the mouth. Diaphragmatic breathing helps to increase blood oxygenation and promote circulation, which can relieve tension in the abdominal muscles and improve digestion. To practice, sit or lie down comfortably, place one hand on your abdomen and the other on your chest. Inhale deeply through your nose, feeling your abdomen expand, and then exhale slowly through your mouth, feeling your abdomen return to its original position. Repeat this practice for a few minutes, concentrating on the feeling of relaxation that accompanies each breath.

Another useful breathing technique is alternate breathing, which helps balance the right and left hemispheres of the brain and reduce stress. To practice alternate breathing, sit comfortably and use your right thumb to close your right nostril. Inhale deeply through your left nostril, then close your left nostril with your ring finger and release your right thumb to exhale through your right nostril. Inhale through the right nostril, close it again with your thumb and exhale through the left nostril. Continue alternating nostrils for a few minutes, maintaining a constant, smooth breathing rhythm.

4-7-8 breathing is another effective technique for promoting relaxation and relieving digestive tension. This practice involves breathing in for four seconds, holding the breath for seven seconds and breathing out slowly for eight seconds. 4-7-8 breathing helps to calm the nervous system and create a state of tranquillity, which is beneficial for digestion. To practice, sit comfortably, close your eyes and follow the 4-7-8 rhythm for several rounds, allowing each breath cycle to bring a sense of calm and balance.

In addition to breathing practices, connecting with nature is a vital component of shamanism and can have a profound impact on digestive health. Spending time outdoors, surrounded by nature, helps to reduce stress and promote a state of general well-being. Nature offers a healing environment that can help balance the mind, body and spirit.

Walking in nature is a simple but powerful practice that can benefit digestive health. Walking in a park, forest or beach allows the body to move naturally, helping to stimulate the digestive system and relieve constipation. In addition, exposure to natural sunlight helps regulate the circadian rhythm, improving sleep quality, which is crucial for digestive health. During your walk, practice mindfulness, observing the sights, sounds and smells around you, and allow nature to calm your mind and body.

The practice of grounding is another effective way to connect with nature and promote digestive health. Grounding involves being in direct contact with the earth, whether by walking barefoot on the grass, sitting on the ground or touching a tree. This practice helps to balance the body's energy and reduce inflammation, which can benefit digestion. To practice grounding, find a quiet spot in nature, take off your shoes and place your feet directly on the earth. Sit or lie down comfortably and focus on the feeling of being connected to the earth, allowing this connection to bring a sense of calm and balance.

Meditation in nature is another powerful practice for digestive health. Meditating outdoors, surrounded by natural beauty, can help deepen the spiritual connection and promote healing. Find a quiet spot in nature, sit comfortably and close your eyes. Focus on your breathing, allowing each inhale and exhale to align with the rhythms of nature around you. Visualize the healing energy of the earth, sky and elements flowing through your body, bringing balance and well-being to the digestive system.

Integrating these practices of breathing and connecting with nature into your daily routine can help relieve digestive symptoms and promote improved overall health. The shamanic approach to healing considers the individual as a whole, treating not only physical symptoms, but also the emotional and spiritual aspects that can contribute to digestive problems. By adopting these practices, it is possible to create a state of balance and harmony that benefits digestive health and general well-being.

Integrating shamanic practices into daily life is crucial to maintaining digestive health and promoting general well-being. Purification techniques, the use of medicinal plants, meditation, breathing and connecting with nature can all be incorporated into a daily routine to create a continuous state of balance and harmony. Here are some practical ways to integrate these practices into everyday life.

Start the day with a purification ritual. Smoking with sacred herbs, such as sage or rosemary, can help cleanse negative energies and prepare the mind and body for the day ahead. When lighting the herbs, keep a clear intention of purification and healing, allowing the smoke to cleanse your space and personal energy. This ritual can be done in a few minutes and can set a positive tone for the day.

Incorporate medicinal plants into your daily diet. Drinking herbal teas such as chamomile, peppermint or ginger can help maintain digestive health. These teas can be consumed throughout the day, especially after meals, to aid digestion and relieve any abdominal discomfort. Also, consider adding fresh herbs to your meals. Herbs such as basil, coriander and fennel not only add flavor to food, but also have digestive properties that can improve gastrointestinal health.

Practice meditation and breathing techniques daily. Taking time to meditate and breathe deeply can help reduce stress and anxiety, which are significant factors in digestive problems. Even if it's just for a few minutes, finding a quiet moment to focus on breathing and meditation can bring significant benefits for digestive health. Consider establishing a morning or evening meditation routine, where you can sit quietly, breathe deeply and visualize the healing energy flowing through your body.

Regular yoga practice can also be beneficial. Incorporating yoga postures that promote digestion and relieve abdominal tension can help maintain digestive health. Postures such as spinal twist, child's pose and cat-cow pose are particularly effective. Take a few minutes in the morning or evening to practice these postures, allowing your body to move and stretch, relieving tension and promoting circulation.

Connect with nature whenever possible. Spending time outdoors, whether walking in a park, gardening or simply sitting in the sun, can have a profound impact on digestive health and overall well-being. Nature offers a healing environment that helps balance the mind, body and spirit. Try to include outdoor activities in your daily routine, allowing yourself to enjoy the healing benefits of nature.

Practice gratitude and mindfulness throughout the day. Taking moments to reflect on the things you are grateful for can help refocus your mind on the positive and reduce stress. Keeping a gratitude journal, where you write down three things you are grateful for each day, can be a powerful practice. In addition, practicing mindfulness, being present in the moment and observing your thoughts and sensations without judgment, can help reduce anxiety and promote a state of calm.

Establish a relaxing evening routine. Preparing for sleep with practices that promote relaxation can help improve sleep quality and, in turn, digestive health. Consider taking a warm bath with lavender or chamomile essential oils, drinking a cup of herbal tea and practicing some breathing techniques or meditation before bed. Creating a peaceful environment free of electronic distractions in the bedroom can also help promote restful sleep.

Practicing self-compassion and self-care is fundamental. Treating yourself with kindness and understanding, especially during times of digestive discomfort, can help relieve stress and anxiety. Recognizing that the journey to healing is continuous and that every step, no matter how small, is progress towards well-being, is essential. Allow yourself time to rest and recharge, and seek support when necessary, whether from friends, family or health professionals.

Integrating these shamanic practices into daily life can create a continuous state of balance and harmony, promoting digestive health and general well-being. By adopting a holistic approach that considers the body, mind and spirit as interconnected, it is possible to achieve deep and lasting healing. The shamanic healing journey is personal and unique, and each practice adopted can contribute to a fuller state of health and a more balanced and harmonious life. Healing chronic pain through shamanism is an ongoing process that involves integrating various holistic practices into daily life. By creating an environment conducive to healing, practicing mindfulness, maintaining a balanced diet, performing light physical exercise and participating in community, it is possible to find relief and promote a better quality of life. These practices not only help to reduce pain, but also promote general well-being, providing a more balanced and harmonious life.

Chapter 8
Respiratory Problems

Respiratory problems are conditions that affect the ability to breathe effectively, impacting the quality of life of many people. These problems can range from acute conditions, such as colds and respiratory infections, to chronic conditions, such as asthma and chronic obstructive pulmonary disease (COPD). Understanding the nature and symptoms of these problems is crucial to addressing them effectively through shamanic practices.

Symptoms of respiratory problems can vary depending on the specific condition, but often include difficulty breathing, shortness of breath, persistent coughing, wheezing, and a feeling of tightness in the chest. In more severe cases, episodes of intense dyspnea, cyanosis (bluish coloration of the skin due to lack of oxygen), and extreme fatigue can occur. Early identification of these symptoms is essential in order to start appropriate treatment and prevent more serious complications.

Respiratory problems can have various causes. Environmental factors, such as exposure to pollutants, allergens and cigarette smoke, are common causes. Respiratory infections, such as flu and pneumonia, also contribute significantly to these problems. In addition, chronic conditions such as asthma and COPD can be triggered or aggravated by genetic factors, sedentary lifestyles and poor diet. Identifying and understanding these causes is fundamental to developing a healing approach that considers all dimensions of the problem.

The shamanic approach to treating respiratory problems involves creating an environment conducive to healing, using relaxation and breathing techniques, and performing healing rituals to restore energy balance. Preparation for the healing ritual begins with the creation of a sacred space in the place where the person spends most of their time. This space should be clean, quiet and free of distractions, promoting an environment that favors relaxation and recovery.

The space can be purified by burning sacred herbs such as sage and rosemary, which have purifying and antibacterial properties. The smoke from these herbs helps to cleanse negative energies and prepare the environment for healing. In addition, the use of healing crystals, such as rose quartz and amethyst, can help relieve respiratory symptoms and promote a sense of peace and well-being.

The regular practice of conscious breathing techniques is a crucial part of shamanic treatment for respiratory problems. Deep, controlled breathing exercises can help open up the airways, improve blood oxygenation and reduce the anxiety associated with breathing difficulties. Techniques such as diaphragmatic breathing, where the breath is concentrated on the expansion of the abdomen, can be particularly effective in relieving tension in the respiratory muscles and promoting a state of relaxation.

In addition to breathing techniques, guided meditation can be a powerful tool for treating respiratory problems. Visualizations of healing light entering the lungs and filling each cell with revitalizing energy can help transform negative energies and promote healing. Meditation can be performed daily, either upon waking or before going to sleep, to reinforce the healing intention and strengthen the spiritual connection.

By integrating these practices into the daily routine, it is possible to create a continuous state of balance and harmony, promoting respiratory health and general well-being. The shamanic approach sees the body, mind and spirit as interconnected, allowing for deep and lasting healing. Each practice adopted can contribute to a fuller state of health and a more balanced and harmonious life, facilitating the recovery and maintenance of respiratory health.

The shamanic approach to respiratory problems involves a series of techniques and practices aimed at relieving symptoms and promoting healing. One of these techniques is the use of medicinal plants and sacred herbs. Herbs such as eucalyptus, mint and thyme have expectorant and anti-inflammatory properties that can help clear the airways and reduce inflammation. Eucalyptus, in particular, is known for its ability to relieve nasal congestion and improve breathing.

Steam inhalation is a traditional practice that can be integrated into shamanic healing. Adding eucalyptus leaves or drops of mint essential oil to a bowl of hot water and inhaling the steam can help to clear the airways and relieve coughs. This ritual can be performed daily or as needed, especially during asthma attacks or cold episodes.

The use of herbal infusions is also effective. Thyme, mint and ginger teas can be consumed to relieve coughs and reduce inflammation. Ginger, in addition to its anti-inflammatory properties, also helps strengthen the immune system, preventing recurrent respiratory infections. Preparing and consuming these teas can be part of a daily ritual that strengthens the connection with nature and promotes healing.

Shamanic healing rituals often involve the use of chants and mantras. Specific chants that invoke healing energy and the protection of nature spirits can be chanted during breathing and meditation practices. The vibration of the chants helps to harmonize the body's energy, promoting a state of peace and balance. Mantras such as "I breathe easily" or "My body is in harmony" can be repeated during meditation to reinforce the healing intention.

Shamanic journeying is a powerful technique that can be used to identify the underlying causes of breathing problems. During the journey, the shaman enters an altered state of consciousness to connect with the guide spirits and gain insights into the patient's condition. The spirit guides can offer guidance on specific healing practices, herbs to use and breathing techniques that may be particularly effective for the individual.

Healing crystals are another important tool in the shamanic treatment of respiratory problems. Amethyst, for example, is known for its calming and purifying properties, helping to relieve the stress and anxiety that can aggravate respiratory problems. Green quartz, on the other hand, is used to promote healing of the lungs and improve respiratory capacity. Placing these crystals in the resting environment or using them during meditation can enhance the healing effects.

The practice of gentle, conscious physical movements, such as tai chi and qigong, can complement shamanic healing techniques. These movements help to improve circulation, strengthen the respiratory muscles and promote flexibility in the chest, making breathing easier. Integrating these practices into the daily routine can not only relieve respiratory symptoms, but also promote general health and well-being.

Herbal baths are another beneficial practice. Adding infusions of eucalyptus, rosemary and lavender to bath water can help relax muscles, relieve tension and promote deep breathing. The combination of steam and the medicinal properties of the herbs creates a healing environment that is both physical and spiritual. This ritual can be especially useful before bed, helping to ensure a restful night's sleep.

The importance of emotional and community support should not be underestimated. Participating in healing circles, where experiences and practices are shared, can provide a sense of belonging and support. These gatherings allow for the exchange of wisdom and strengthen the determination to continue with healing practices. The support of a community that understands and validates the healing journey can be a powerful catalyst for recovery.

Shamanic healing emphasizes the importance of connecting with nature and guardian spirits in promoting respiratory health. The belief that all life forms are interconnected and possess a vital energy is central to shamanic practice. Integrating spiritual practices that reinforce this connection can be a powerful tool in healing respiratory problems.

One such practice is the creation of an outdoor altar. Choosing a place in nature, such as a garden or a quiet area in a park, to set up an altar can provide a sacred space for meditation and healing rituals. The altar can include elements from nature, such as stones, shells, feathers, and medicinal plants that symbolize the healing intention. Performing rituals in this space can strengthen the connection with nature spirits and amplify the healing power of shamanic practices.

Nature walks are another recommended practice. Walking in forests, mountains or along rivers not only improves physical health, but also promotes mental and spiritual peace. Breathing in the fresh air and observing the natural beauty around you can help release tension and promote a sense of well-being. During these walks, you can practice mindfulness, focusing on breathing and the sounds of nature, which helps to calm the mind and improve breathing capacity.

The practice of gratitude is a spiritual technique that can have a profound impact on healing. Taking a moment every day to express gratitude for life, health and nature can transform the mindset and promote feelings of peace and contentment. Gratitude helps to focus the mind on the positive, reducing stress and promoting inner harmony. Writing in a gratitude journal or verbalizing thanks during meditation can be a powerful practice to support respiratory healing.

The use of music and natural sounds during meditation and healing rituals can create an atmosphere of tranquillity and facilitate spiritual connection. Soothing sounds, such as birdsong, the sound of rain, or the flow of a stream, can be played during meditation to create a relaxing atmosphere. Playing shamanic musical instruments, such as drums and flutes, can also help induce altered states of consciousness and facilitate the spiritual journey.

Purification ceremonies are essential practices in shamanic healing. One such ceremony is the sacred sauna, known as the sweat lodge. This ritual involves creating an enclosed space where heated stones are used to generate steam, symbolizing the purification of the body and spirit. During the ceremony, the shaman may lead chants and prayers, helping to release physical and energetic toxins and promoting deep healing. The sweat lodge is a practice that requires preparation and should be conducted by an experienced shaman to ensure the safety and effectiveness of the ritual.

Sacred herbal baths are another form of purification that can be integrated into the healing routine. Preparing an infusion of herbs such as rosemary, eucalyptus and lavender and adding it to the bath water can help relax the respiratory muscles and promote deep breathing. This ritual can be performed weekly or as needed, creating a space for self-care and continuous healing.

The integration of visualization practices is fundamental to shamanic healing. During meditation, visualizing a healing light entering the lungs and filling the whole body with vital energy can help transform negative energies and promote healing. Visualizing yourself breathing easily and freely can reinforce the healing intention and strengthen the mind and spirit. This practice can be done daily, especially before bed, to relax the body and mind.

The use of amulets and talismans can also be incorporated into healing practices. These sacred objects, charged with the intention of protection and healing, can be worn or placed in the resting environment. Amulets made from stones such as black tourmaline, known for their protective properties, can help create a safe energy field, protecting against negative influences that could affect respiratory health.

By integrating these spiritual practices and connecting with nature, it is possible to promote holistic healing that encompasses the body, mind and spirit. Shamanic healing for respiratory problems is not just about relieving physical symptoms, but also about restoring harmony and balance in all aspects of life. These practices offer a path to improved respiratory health and general well-being, providing a fuller and more conscious life.

Shamanic healing for respiratory problems also emphasizes the importance of a balanced diet and healthy lifestyle habits. Proper nutrition plays a crucial role in maintaining respiratory health and strengthening the immune system. Integrating nutrient-rich foods and avoiding substances that can aggravate respiratory symptoms are essential practices for effective healing.

Anti-inflammatory foods are particularly beneficial for those suffering from respiratory problems. Fruits and vegetables rich in antioxidants, such as berries, spinach, broccoli and carrots, help to reduce inflammation in the body and improve respiratory function. Foods rich in omega-3 fatty acids, such as salmon, chia seeds and walnuts, are also known for their anti-inflammatory properties and can help relieve the symptoms of asthma and other respiratory conditions.

Adequate hydration is fundamental to respiratory health. Drinking plenty of water helps to keep the airways hydrated and facilitate the elimination of mucus and toxins from the body. Herbal teas, such as chamomile, ginger and mint, not only help with hydration, but also offer calming and anti-inflammatory benefits. Avoiding drinks that can dehydrate, such as coffee and alcohol, is important for maintaining respiratory health.

Foods that strengthen the immune system are also essential. Garlic, for example, has antibacterial and antiviral properties that can help prevent respiratory infections. Honey is another powerful food, known for its antibacterial and anti-inflammatory properties, which can relieve coughs and sore throats. Integrating these foods into the daily diet can significantly contribute to maintaining respiratory health.

In addition to diet, regular moderate physical exercise is crucial for improving lung function and respiratory capacity. Activities such as walking, swimming and yoga not only strengthen the respiratory muscles, but also help to reduce stress and anxiety, which can aggravate respiratory problems. Breathing exercises, such as pranayama in yoga, are particularly effective for improving respiratory efficiency and promoting calm.

Sleep hygiene is another vital aspect of respiratory health. Ensuring a suitable sleeping environment, free of allergens and with good ventilation, is essential. Using hypoallergenic pillows, washing bed linen regularly and avoiding exposure to irritants such as dust and smoke can help prevent respiratory problems during the night. Maintaining a consistent sleep routine and ensuring that you get enough sleep is also important for recovery and maintaining overall health.

Stress reduction is an integral part of shamanic healing, as chronic stress can weaken the immune system and aggravate respiratory symptoms. Relaxation practices such as meditation, mindfulness and visualization techniques help to reduce stress and promote a state of inner peace. Integrating moments of pause and self-care into the daily routine is essential for maintaining balance and health.

The importance of avoiding harmful substances cannot be underestimated. Avoiding smoking, both active and passive, is crucial for respiratory health. Exposure to toxic chemicals, such as aggressive cleaning products and environmental pollutants, should be minimized wherever possible. Opting for natural products and keeping the home well ventilated can help reduce exposure to these substances.

Practicing daily rituals that promote respiratory health can make a big difference. Starting the day with a guided meditation focused on breathing, drinking a calming herbal tea, and taking a walk outdoors are simple practices that can strengthen respiratory health. Creating a sacred space at home where you can practice these activities can reinforce the healing intention and provide an atmosphere of peace and rejuvenation.

Integrating a healthy diet, balanced lifestyle habits and spiritual practices is essential for the shamanic healing of respiratory problems. These holistic practices not only relieve physical symptoms, but also promote emotional and spiritual health, providing a complete and lasting cure. By following these guidelines, it is possible to achieve a healthier, more balanced and fulfilling life, with strengthened respiratory health and a deeper connection with nature and spirit.

Shamanic healing for respiratory problems is an ongoing process that requires the integration of various practices and healthy lifestyle habits. Maintaining long-term respiratory health involves adopting routines that reinforce physical, emotional and spiritual well-being. The key to lasting healing is consistency and adapting these practices to everyday life, ensuring that they become an integral part of daily life.

An essential practice is keeping a healing journal. Recording daily practices, food consumed, meditations performed and symptoms observed can provide a clear view of progress and help identify patterns that may influence respiratory health. The diary also serves as a space for personal reflections, notes of gratitude and insights gained during shamanic practices.

Adapting conscious breathing practices is crucial for maintaining respiratory health. Techniques such as diaphragmatic breathing and alternate breathing should be incorporated into the daily routine. Taking a few minutes in the morning and evening to practice these exercises can help keep the airways open and promote proper oxygenation of the body. These practices not only improve lung function, but also help to reduce stress and anxiety.

Meditation remains a powerful tool for respiratory health. Guided meditations focused on breathing, healing light visualizations and shamanic chanting should be practiced regularly. Integrating meditation into the daily routine, whether waking up or before bed, helps maintain calm, mental clarity and spiritual connection, all of which are essential for robust respiratory health.

Participating in healing circles and shamanic workshops can provide a sense of community and ongoing support. Sharing experiences, learning new healing techniques and receiving guidance from experienced shamans enriches the healing journey. These gatherings not only offer emotional support, but also broaden knowledge about shamanic practices and healing methods.

The importance of regularly connecting with nature cannot be underestimated. Spending time outdoors, whether through hiking, gardening or simply sitting in a park, promotes respiratory health and general well-being. Nature has a calming and revitalizing effect, and being in contact with it regularly helps maintain energy balance. Practicing mindfulness in nature, observing the sounds, colors and smells around you, can be a powerful form of meditation and reconnection with the natural environment.

Regular physical exercise should be maintained to strengthen the respiratory muscles and improve lung capacity. Activities such as yoga, tai chi and swimming are highly recommended, as they combine physical movement with conscious breathing techniques. These exercises not only improve physical health, but also promote mental peace and emotional balance.

Diet continues to play a vital role in maintaining respiratory health. Consuming a diet rich in fruits, vegetables, whole grains and lean proteins provides the nutrients needed to support the immune system and reduce inflammation. Incorporating superfoods such as turmeric, ginger and antioxidant-rich fruits can help fight free radicals and promote healing. Avoiding processed foods, refined sugars and trans fats is crucial to keeping the body in balance and avoiding chronic inflammation.

The importance of hydration should always be remembered. Staying well hydrated is essential for proper respiratory function, as water helps to keep the mucous membranes of the airways moist, making breathing easier. Drinking water throughout the day, as well as consuming calming herbal teas, can help maintain hydration and promote respiratory health.

Finally, the practice of gratitude and self-compassion should be integrated into daily life. Taking a moment each day to reflect on the things you are grateful for can transform your mindset and promote a sense of contentment and peace. Treating yourself with kindness and understanding, especially during times of difficulty, is fundamental to emotional and spiritual healing. Self-compassion involves recognizing one's own efforts and progress, and accepting that the healing journey is an ongoing process.

In summary, maintaining respiratory health through shamanic healing is an ongoing commitment to practices that promote balance and harmony in all aspects of life. Integrating breathing exercises, meditation, healthy eating, physical exercise and spiritual practices into the daily routine helps to strengthen respiratory health and promote general well-being. By following these guidelines and adapting the practices to your own life, you can achieve lasting healing and live a fuller, more conscious life, with robust respiratory health and a deep connection to nature and spirit.

Chapter 9
Circulatory Problems

Circulatory problems represent a common condition that can significantly affect quality of life. These problems include poor circulation, hypertension, arteriosclerosis and peripheral vascular disease. Typical symptoms are pain and tiredness in the legs, swelling, varicose veins, tingling sensations or numbness, and changes in skin color. Identifying these symptoms early is crucial to avoiding serious complications.

One of the most frequent causes of circulatory problems is poor diet. Diets rich in saturated fats, sugars and processed foods can lead to plaque build-up in the arteries, restricting blood flow. Lack of physical activity also contributes significantly, as regular exercise helps keep blood vessels flexible and promotes healthy blood flow.

Stress and anxiety are additional factors that can negatively affect circulation. The body responds to chronic stress by releasing hormones such as cortisol, which can cause inflammation and negatively affect the cardiovascular system. Shamanic practice recognizes the importance of addressing these emotional and mental factors alongside the physical aspects of illness.

The shamanic approach to treating circulatory problems involves creating an environment conducive to healing and using practices that promote the circulation of vital energy. A sacred space should be created, free from distractions and filled with objects that symbolize healing and vitality, such as crystals, herbs and spiritual symbols. The atmosphere can be enriched by burning herbs such as sage and using essential oils known for their circulation-promoting properties, such as rosemary and mint.

Meditation and visualization are essential tools in shamanic practice. During meditation, the practitioner can visualize vital energy flowing freely through the body, dissolving blockages and promoting a healthy flow. Visualizing healing light moving along the veins and arteries can help reinforce the healing intention and improve circulation.

Healing rituals can include the use of specific crystals known for their circulation-promoting properties. Rose quartz, for example, is often used to improve blood flow and promote cardiovascular health. Placing these crystals on the body's energy points during meditation can help dissolve blockages and restore energy flow.

Regular gentle physical exercise, such as walking and yoga, is recommended to improve circulation. These activities help strengthen the cardiovascular system and promote healthy blood flow. In addition, deep breathing techniques can help reduce stress and anxiety, improving the overall health of the circulatory system.

A balanced diet rich in fruit, vegetables, whole grains and healthy fats is essential for maintaining cardiovascular health. Foods such as garlic, ginger and turmeric are known for their anti-inflammatory properties and can be incorporated into the diet to promote blood circulation. Drinking plenty of water is equally important to keep the blood flowing freely through the body.

Massage therapy can also be an effective tool for treating circulatory problems. Massage techniques that focus on stimulating blood flow can help relieve pain and swelling, promoting a general feeling of well-being. Applying essential oils during the massage can enhance these benefits, providing a complete healing experience.

Integrating these practices into everyday life can help maintain circulatory health and prevent the development of more serious problems. The shamanic approach, with its holistic focus, seeks to treat not only the physical symptoms, but also the underlying emotional and mental causes of circulatory problems, promoting complete and lasting healing.

In addition to meditation and visualization practices, shamanic healing rituals can involve the use of sounds and vibrations to promote blood circulation. The use of drums, rattles and other rhythmic instruments can help stimulate the flow of energy through the body, promoting circulation and dissolving energy blockages. The rhythmic beat of the drum, in particular, is known for its ability to induce trance states and facilitate deep healing.

Medicinal herbs play a significant role in the shamanic healing of circulatory problems. Herbs such as ginkgo biloba, horsetail and witch hazel are known for their properties in strengthening blood vessels and improving circulation. These herbs can be prepared as teas or infusions and incorporated into the daily routine to support cardiovascular health. The use of herbal poultices applied directly to the skin can also help relieve the pain and swelling associated with circulatory problems.

The practice of immersion baths with herbs and essential oils is another effective technique in the shamanic approach. Baths with the addition of rosemary, peppermint and eucalyptus oil can help stimulate circulation and relax muscles. Hot water improves the dilation of blood vessels, facilitating better blood flow and promoting detoxification of the body.

Connecting with nature is a central element in shamanic practice, and can be particularly beneficial for people with circulatory problems. Walks in nature, especially in areas with lots of greenery, not only provide physical exercise, but also help to reduce stress and improve emotional well-being. Sitting next to a flowing body of water or in a quiet woodland can help balance the body's energy and promote healing.

In addition, the practice of grounding can be extremely beneficial. Walking barefoot on earth or grass helps to connect the body with the energies of the earth, promoting an energetic balance and helping to reduce inflammation. This simple practice can be incorporated into the daily routine to maintain circulatory health.

Conscious eating is fundamental in the shamanic approach to circulatory problems. A diet rich in nutrients and low in processed foods can help keep arteries clean and flexible. Incorporating anti-inflammatory foods, such as berries, nuts and seeds, can help reduce inflammation and improve circulation. Regular consumption of omega-3 fatty acids, found in oily fish and flaxseeds, is also highly beneficial for cardiovascular health.

Specific breathing practices, such as abdominal or diaphragmatic breathing, are effective for improving blood oxygenation and promoting circulation. Conscious breathing helps reduce stress, which in turn can have a positive effect on blood pressure and heart health. Dedicating a few minutes a day to practicing breathing techniques can make a significant difference to circulatory health.

Sound therapy, which uses specific frequencies to promote healing, is an additional technique that can be used. Specific tones and vibrations can help dissolve energy blockages and improve blood flow. The use of Tibetan bowls and tuning forks can be integrated into healing sessions to promote circulatory health.

Integrating these various practices into daily life can help create a continuous state of balance and well-being. The shamanic approach to circulatory problems is holistic, treating not only the physical symptoms, but also addressing the underlying emotional and mental causes. This integrated approach promotes complete and lasting healing, improving quality of life and preventing future complications.

Shamanic practice also includes therapeutic massage techniques to improve circulation. Massage can help stimulate blood flow, relieve muscle tension and promote lymphatic drainage. Techniques such as hot stone massage and reflexology are particularly effective for treating circulatory problems. Hot stones help dilate blood vessels, facilitating better blood flow, while reflexology works on specific points on the feet that correspond to different organs and systems in the body, promoting circulation and energy balance.

Hydrotherapy is another valuable practice in the shamanic approach to circulatory problems. Alternating between hot and cold baths can help stimulate blood circulation and strengthen blood vessels. Contrast baths, where you alternate between hot and cold water, can be done at home and are effective for improving circulation in the legs and feet. This simple but powerful technique can be incorporated into your daily routine to promote cardiovascular health.

Regular exercise is essential for maintaining a healthy circulatory system. Light to moderate aerobic activities, such as walking, swimming or cycling, are highly recommended. These exercises help strengthen the heart, improve circulation and keep blood vessels flexible. In addition, specific stretching exercises can help improve flexibility and blood circulation in muscles and joints.

Conscious breathing and relaxation techniques are essential for reducing stress, which is a significant factor in circulatory problems. Practices such as mindfulness meditation, yoga and tai chi can help reduce stress and anxiety levels, promoting a general sense of well-being. Diaphragmatic breathing, which focuses on breathing deeply through the abdomen, can be practiced several times a day to relax the body and mind.

The use of healing crystals remains an important practice. In addition to rose quartz, crystals such as hematite and carnelian are known for their circulation-boosting properties. Hematite is often used to increase strength and vitality, while carnelian helps to stimulate blood circulation and vital energy. These crystals can be worn during meditation or carried throughout the day to support circulatory health.

Acupressure is another effective technique that can be integrated into shamanic practice. This technique involves applying pressure to specific points on the body to relieve tension and improve blood flow. Points such as Stomach Point 36 (ST36) and Spleen Point 6 (SP6) are known for their circulation-promoting properties and can be massaged regularly to support cardiovascular health.

Diet is a crucial aspect of the holistic approach to circulatory problems. Incorporating foods rich in antioxidants, such as citrus fruits, dark leafy greens and berries, can help protect blood vessels and improve circulation. Foods rich in fiber, such as whole grains, help maintain healthy cholesterol levels, reducing the risk of atherosclerosis. Avoiding processed and sodium-rich foods is also important to prevent fluid retention and increased blood pressure.

The practice of intermittent fasting can be explored as a technique for improving cardiovascular health. Intermittent fasting involves regular periods of fasting followed by eating. This practice can help reduce inflammation, improve insulin sensitivity and promote heart health. However, it is important to consult a health professional before starting any fasting regime.

Community support is essential in the healing process. Participating in support groups or healing circles can provide a sense of belonging and emotional support. Sharing experiences and practices with others facing circulatory problems can offer new insights and strengthen the resolve to follow healing practices. Community can provide a safe and welcoming environment to explore and integrate new healing techniques.

The shamanic approach to circulatory problems is comprehensive and integrated, addressing all aspects of being - physical, emotional and spiritual. By incorporating practices such as massage therapy, hydrotherapy, conscious breathing and a balanced diet, it is possible to promote complete and lasting healing. These practices not only improve circulatory health, but also promote general well-being, providing a more balanced and harmonious life.

Circulatory problems, when approached holistically, consider the importance of maintaining a balance between body, mind and spirit. Shamanic practice emphasizes the integration of various techniques to promote circulatory health and prevent complications. One of these techniques is the practice of conscious movement, such as Qigong and Tai Chi, which are ancient arts known for their benefits in improving circulation and promoting the flow of vital energy, or "qi".

Qigong and Tai Chi involve slow, controlled movements combined with deep breathing and mental concentration. These exercises help to open up the energy channels in the body, promoting more efficient blood circulation and balancing internal energies. Regular practice of these arts can reduce stress, improve flexibility and increase physical endurance, contributing to cardiovascular health.

Phytotherapy is another valuable approach in shamanic practice for treating circulatory problems. In addition to the herbs mentioned above, other plants such as horse chestnut, turmeric and garlic are known for their beneficial properties for circulation. Horse chestnut, for example, is effective in strengthening veins and preventing varicose veins. Turmeric has anti-inflammatory and anticoagulant properties, helping to keep the blood flowing freely. Garlic is known for its ability to lower blood pressure and improve arterial health. These herbs can be incorporated into the daily diet or used in supplement form under the guidance of a health professional.

The practice of aromatherapy can also be integrated into the healing routine. Essential oils such as cypress, ginger and lemon are especially useful for improving circulation. Cypress oil is known for its vasoconstrictive properties, helping to strengthen the walls of blood vessels. Ginger warms the body and promotes blood flow, while lemon helps to detoxify the system and improve circulation. These oils can be used in massages, added to baths or diffused in the environment to obtain their therapeutic benefits.

The use of contrast baths, alternating between hot and cold water, is an effective technique for stimulating blood circulation. Hot water dilates the blood vessels, while cold water constricts them, creating a pumping effect that improves blood flow and relieves muscle tension. This simple practice can be carried out at home, incorporating essential oils to increase its benefits.

The energy of sound and vibration also plays an important role in shamanic healing. Instruments such as drums, rattles and Tibetan bowls can be used to create vibrations that promote circulation and balance the body's energies. The resonance of these vibrations can help release energy blockages, promoting healthy blood flow and a general sense of well-being.

Conscious breathing is a powerful technique for improving circulation. Deep breathing exercises, such as diaphragmatic breathing, help oxygenate the blood and relax the body. Regular practice of breathing techniques can reduce stress and anxiety, improving cardiovascular health. One effective exercise is 4-7-8 breathing, which involves breathing in through the nose for 4 seconds, holding the breath for 7 seconds and exhaling slowly through the mouth for 8 seconds. This practice can be done several times a day to promote calm and balance.

Conscious eating remains fundamental in maintaining a healthy circulatory system. Foods rich in antioxidants, such as citrus fruits, berries and green leafy vegetables, help protect blood vessels and improve circulation. Incorporating healthy fats, such as those found in avocados, nuts and olive oil, can help reduce inflammation and promote heart health. Avoiding processed and sodium-rich foods is crucial to prevent fluid retention and high blood pressure.

In addition to diet, adequate hydration is essential. Drinking enough water throughout the day helps keep the blood flowing and facilitates the transportation of nutrients and oxygen throughout the body. Dehydration can lead to a decrease in blood volume, hindering circulation and increasing the risk of cardiovascular problems.

The practice of yoga can be particularly beneficial for circulatory health. Specific yoga poses, such as the downward facing dog pose (Adho Mukha Svanasana) and the legs up the wall pose (Viparita Karani), help to improve blood circulation and reduce swelling in the legs. The combination of stretching, deep breathing and relaxation found in yoga helps to reduce stress and strengthen the cardiovascular system.

Practicing gratitude rituals and meditation can help maintain a positive mental state, which is crucial for general health. Gratitude and regular meditation can reduce stress levels and promote a state of calm, directly benefiting heart health and blood circulation. Taking time every day to reflect on the things you are grateful for can transform your outlook on life and improve your emotional well-being.

The importance of social and community support should not be underestimated. Taking part in healing circles, meditation groups or other spiritual communities can provide a sense of belonging and emotional support. Sharing experiences and practices with others who are on the same journey can offer new insights and strengthen the resolve to maintain healing practices.

The shamanic approach to circulatory problems is deeply holistic, integrating body, mind and spirit. By adopting practices such as conscious movement, herbal medicine, aromatherapy, conscious breathing, healthy eating and relaxation techniques, it is possible to promote complete and lasting healing. These practices not only improve circulatory health, but also promote general well-being, providing a more balanced and harmonious life.

The shamanic approach to treating circulatory problems is multifaceted and involves diverse techniques that consider all aspects of the being. One effective and accessible practice is self-massage. Self-massage can be done daily, using essential oils such as rosemary and ginger, known for their circulation-stimulating properties. Gentle, firm circular movements can help stimulate blood flow and relieve tension in the muscles.

In addition to self-massage, the use of suction cups is a traditional technique that can be beneficial. The application of suction cups creates a gentle suction on the skin, which can help improve blood circulation and release toxins from the body. This technique, although simple, should be carried out with care and preferably under the guidance of an experienced professional.

Stretching exercises are essential for keeping muscles flexible and promoting circulation. Specific exercises, such as leg and arm stretches, help improve blood flow to the extremities, preventing blood stagnation. Daily stretches can be incorporated into the morning or evening routine to keep muscles healthy and improve circulation.

Spiritual connection and meditation remain important pillars in the shamanic approach. Meditations that focus on the circulation of energy through the body can be especially useful. During meditation, visualize the vital energy flowing through your veins and arteries, dissolving any blockages and promoting a healthy flow. This practice not only improves blood circulation, but also promotes a state of inner peace and balance.

Earthing is a simple but powerful technique that involves walking barefoot on the earth. This practice helps connect the body to the energies of the earth, promoting an energetic balance and improving circulation. Spending time outdoors, especially in green areas, can help reduce stress and improve cardiovascular health.

The role of diet in circulatory health cannot be underestimated. In addition to a diet rich in fruit, vegetables, whole grains and healthy fats, it is important to avoid foods that contribute to inflammation and the build-up of plaque in the arteries. Reducing your intake of sugar, salt and processed foods can help keep your arteries clean and flexible. Foods rich in magnesium, such as nuts, seeds and dark leafy greens, are especially beneficial for cardiovascular health.

The importance of adequate hydration is also crucial. Keeping the body well hydrated helps to ensure that the blood remains fluid, facilitating circulation. Dehydration can lead to the formation of blood clots and other circulatory problems, so it is essential to drink enough water throughout the day.

Regular physical exercise, such as walking, swimming and cycling, helps keep the heart healthy and promotes good circulation. These exercises not only strengthen the cardiovascular system, but also help to reduce stress and anxiety, factors that can negatively affect circulation. Incorporating physical activity into the daily routine is fundamental to overall health.

Phytotherapy continues to be an important practice in the shamanic approach to circulatory problems. In addition to the herbs already mentioned, plants such as hibiscus and olive are also known for their cardiovascular benefits. Hibiscus tea can help reduce blood pressure, while olive leaf extract can improve arterial function and reduce the risk of heart disease.

Sound therapy, using instruments such as Tibetan bowls and wind chimes, can help create a state of deep relaxation and promote the circulation of energy throughout the body. The resonance of these vibrations can help release energy blockages and improve blood flow, promoting a general state of well-being.

The shamanic approach to treating circulatory problems is comprehensive and holistic, integrating various techniques and practices to promote health and well-being. By incorporating self-massage practices, stretching exercises, meditation, grounding, healthy eating and adequate hydration, it is possible to improve circulation and prevent future complications. These practices not only improve physical health, but also promote emotional and spiritual balance, providing a more harmonious and healthy life.

Chapter 10
Skin Problems

Skin problems are common conditions that can affect people of all ages. These problems range from mild to severe and can have a significant impact on the quality of life and self-esteem of those affected. The skin is the largest organ in the human body and serves as a protective barrier against external agents, as well as playing a crucial role in regulating body temperature and sensory perception.

Symptoms of skin problems can be varied and include rashes, redness, itching, dryness, peeling, blistering, open sores and changes in skin pigmentation. These conditions can be caused by a number of factors, including allergies, infections, autoimmune diseases, genetics, exposure to environmental irritants and poor eating habits.

Allergies are a common cause of skin problems and can be triggered by substances such as pollen, food, medicines, personal care products and clothing materials. Allergic reactions on the skin can manifest as hives, contact dermatitis or atopic eczema, which are characterized by red, itchy rashes.

Skin infections can be caused by bacteria, viruses, fungi or parasites. Common examples include impetigo (caused by bacteria), herpes (caused by viruses), mycoses (caused by fungi) and scabies (caused by mites). These infections can lead to a variety of symptoms, such as blisters, scabs, ulcers and intense itching, depending on the infectious agent involved.

Autoimmune diseases, such as psoriasis and lupus, can cause chronic inflammation and skin changes. Psoriasis manifests as thick, scaly plaques, while lupus can cause a butterfly-shaped rash on the face and other skin lesions on various parts of the body.

Genetics also plays an important role in many skin problems. Some conditions, such as eczema and rosacea, can be hereditary and tend to run in families. In addition, genetic factors can influence the body's response to environmental irritants and infectious agents, increasing predisposition to skin problems.

Exposure to environmental irritants such as chemicals, pollution, ultraviolet radiation and extreme weather can damage the skin and cause inflammation. For example, prolonged exposure to the sun without adequate protection can lead to sunburn, premature skin ageing and increase the risk of skin cancer.

Poor eating habits, including diets low in essential nutrients, can compromise skin health. A deficiency of vitamins and minerals, such as vitamins A, C, E and zinc, can affect the skin's ability to regenerate and protect itself against damage. In addition, excessive consumption of processed foods, sugars and fats can contribute to the development of acne and other inflammatory skin conditions.

The shamanic approach to treating skin problems involves a combination of spiritual practices, the use of medicinal plants and energy healing techniques. Preparing for rituals is a crucial step that helps create a sacred environment conducive to healing.

Preparing the sacred space is essential. Choose a quiet place where there are no interruptions. Physically clean the space and use sacred herbs such as sage, cedar or palo santo for energetic purification. Smoking the space with these herbs helps to remove negative energies and creates an environment conducive to healing. It's important to set a clear intention before starting the ritual, focusing on healing and the well-being of the skin.

Creating a personal altar is a fundamental step in the preparation. The altar can include elements that symbolize the healing intention, such as crystals, candles, medicinal plants and spiritual symbols. Crystals such as amethyst and rose quartz are particularly beneficial for skin problems due to their soothing and healing properties. Amethyst is known for its ability to relieve stress and purify energy, while rose quartz promotes self-love and emotional healing.

Shamanic journeying is a powerful technique for accessing spiritual insights and promoting healing. To begin the journey, sit comfortably and start with a deep meditation. Use the rhythmic sound of a drum or rattle to enter an altered state of consciousness. Visualize yourself in a sacred place in nature, where you feel safe and protected. Invite your spirit guides and power animals to accompany you on this journey. Ask for guidance on the causes of skin problems and suitable healing methods.

During the journey, you may meet nature spirits who offer wisdom and support. They can show you which medicinal plants to use or which rituals to perform to promote healing. Communicating with these spirits is a vital part of the shamanic healing process. Thank them for their guidance and take note of the messages you receive to apply to your healing practice.

In addition to the shamanic journey, the application of medicinal plants is a traditional and effective practice for skin problems. Plants such as calendula, aloe vera and lavender have anti-inflammatory, antimicrobial and regenerative properties that help treat a variety of skin conditions. Calendula, for example, can be used in the form of an ointment or infusion to relieve inflammation and promote healing. Aloe vera gel is known for its moisturizing and soothing properties and is ideal for treating burns and irritations. Lavender essential oil can be applied topically to reduce redness and promote skin regeneration.

Bath rituals with medicinal herbs are another effective technique. Prepare a warm bath and add herbal infusions such as chamomile, calendula and lavender. Immerse yourself in the bath, visualizing the water as a healing agent that cleanses and revitalizes the skin. While in the bath, practice deep, relaxing breathing, allowing your mind and body to calm down.

The practice of gratitude and self-acceptance is fundamental to the healing process. Skin problems are often linked to feelings of shame or low self-esteem. Incorporating daily gratitude rituals can help transform these negative emotions into positive ones. Give thanks for your body's ability to heal and regenerate, and visualize yourself with healthy, radiant skin.

In addition, connecting with the elements of nature can be deeply healing. Spend time outdoors, enjoying the revitalizing energy of the sun, earth, water and air. Walking barefoot on earth or grass, known as grounding, helps balance the body's energy and promotes a sense of well-being.

Energy healing is an essential part of shamanic practices for treating skin problems. This approach involves the manipulation of subtle energies to promote balance and regeneration of the skin. Below, we explore some specific energy healing techniques and visualizations that can be integrated into daily rituals.

One of the most widely used energy healing techniques is the laying on of hands. This practice involves channeling healing energy through the hands to the affected areas of the skin. To begin, find a quiet space where you can concentrate without interruption. Sit or lie down comfortably and close your eyes. Start with a few deep breaths to relax your body and mind.

Place your hands on the area of skin that needs healing. Visualize a white or golden light flowing through your hands and entering the skin. Feel this energy as warmth or a slight vibration. Focus on the intention of healing and regeneration, allowing the energy to flow freely. Hold this visualization for 10 to 15 minutes, or until you feel the energy has stabilized.

The practice of visualizations is another powerful technique for promoting skin health. An effective visualization involves imagining the affected skin being enveloped in a healing light. Close your eyes and take a few deep breaths. Visualize a bright golden or white light coming down from the universe and enveloping your entire body. Focus this light especially on the areas of the skin that need healing. Imagine the light penetrating the layers of the skin, repairing damaged cells, reducing inflammation and promoting regeneration.

Another visualization technique involves imagining healthy, radiant skin. Visualize yourself in a mirror, seeing your perfectly healthy, smooth and radiant skin. Feel the joy and gratitude of this image and hold this visualization for a few minutes every day. This practice helps reprogram the mind and body to accept and manifest healing.

Crystal healing is another effective shamanic practice. Each crystal has unique energetic properties that can benefit the skin. In addition to the use of amethyst and rose quartz mentioned above, other crystals such as black tourmaline, selenite and green aventurine can be used. Black tourmaline helps protect against negative energies, selenite promotes energetic cleansing, and green aventurine is known for its healing properties.

To use crystals for skin healing, you can place them directly on the affected area or hold them while performing meditations and visualizations. Clean the crystals regularly to ensure that their energy remains pure and effective. This can be done by running them under running water, leaving them in sunlight or moonlight, or using other purification techniques.

The practice of grounding is another important technique. Connecting directly with the earth helps to balance the body's energies and promote healing. Spend time outdoors, walking barefoot on grass, sand or earth. Feel the energy of the earth rising through your feet and filling your whole body. This practice not only benefits the skin, but also promotes general well-being.

Conscious breathing is essential for energy healing. Deep, controlled breathing practices help to oxygenate the blood and promote circulation, which is vital for skin health. One effective technique is alternate breathing, where you inhale through one nostril, hold your breath and exhale through the other nostril. This practice helps to balance the energies in the body and reduce stress, which is a contributing factor to many skin problems.

Music and healing sounds can be integrated into healing rituals. The use of drums, rattles and shamanic chants helps to create a healing atmosphere and raise the energetic vibration. Singing or listening to healing music while performing laying on of hands practices or visualizations can amplify the healing effects.

Diet and daily skin care play a crucial role in maintaining skin health and the effectiveness of shamanic healing practices. A holistic approach that includes a balanced diet and proper skin care habits can complement energy healing rituals and techniques, promoting complete and lasting regeneration.

Nutrition is fundamental to skin health. A diet rich in fruits, vegetables, whole grains, lean proteins and healthy fats provides the essential nutrients the skin needs to regenerate and protect itself against damage. Foods rich in antioxidants, such as berries, nuts and seeds, help fight free radicals that can damage skin cells. Vitamins A, C, E and minerals such as zinc are particularly important for skin health.

Vitamin A, found in foods such as carrots, pumpkin and spinach, is crucial for cell renewal and tissue repair. Vitamin C, found in citrus fruits, peppers and broccoli, is essential for the production of collagen, which keeps the skin firm and elastic. Vitamin E, found in nuts, seeds and vegetable oils, has antioxidant properties that protect the skin against environmental damage. Zinc, found in foods such as nuts, seeds and legumes, helps regulate immune function and skin healing.

Staying hydrated is equally important. Water is vital for keeping the skin hydrated and helping to eliminate toxins from the body. Drinking at least eight glasses of water a day can make a significant difference to the appearance and health of the skin. Herbal teas, such as green tea and chamomile tea, can also be beneficial due to their antioxidant and anti-inflammatory properties.

In addition to diet, daily skin care is essential to promote healing and regeneration. Proper skin cleansing helps to remove impurities, oil and dead cells that can clog pores and cause skin problems. Use gentle, natural cleansers that don't irritate the skin.

Avoid products that contain harsh chemicals, artificial fragrances or alcohol, as they can cause irritation and dryness.

Regular exfoliation, once or twice a week, helps to remove dead skin cells and promote cell renewal. Use natural exfoliants, such as sugar, sea salt or ground oats, mixed with vegetable oils for a gentle and effective scrub. Avoid aggressive scrubs that can cause micro-injuries to the skin.

Moisturizing is key to maintaining healthy skin and preventing dryness and irritation. Use natural moisturizers, such as coconut, jojoba and almond oils, which nourish and protect the skin. Apply the moisturizer right after showering, when the skin is still damp, to seal in the moisture.

Sun protection is another crucial part of daily skin care. Excessive exposure to the sun can cause damage to the skin, such as burns, premature ageing and an increased risk of skin cancer. Use natural sunscreens with zinc oxide or titanium dioxide, which offer effective protection against UV rays without harmful chemicals. Reapply sunscreen every two hours when outdoors.

Practicing relaxation and stress reduction techniques is also vital for skin health. Stress can aggravate many skin conditions, such as acne, eczema and psoriasis. Practices such as meditation, yoga and deep breathing help to reduce stress levels and promote a state of relaxation that benefits the skin.

Incorporating self-care rituals into your daily routine can have a profound impact on skin health. Set aside time every day to take care of yourself, whether it's through a relaxing bath, a facial massage with essential oils or a guided meditation. These rituals not only benefit the skin, but also promote general well-being and a connection with the inner self.

In addition, it is important to be patient and consistent with skin care. Skin regeneration and healing can take time, and the results may not be immediate. Maintaining a consistent routine of skin care and energy healing practices, along with a healthy diet, is the key to achieving and maintaining healthy, radiant skin.

Integrating shamanic healing practices and daily skin care into a holistic lifestyle is essential to achieving and maintaining optimal skin health. This approach involves creating a harmonious balance between body, mind and spirit, promoting general well-being and continuous skin regeneration.

One of the first steps to integrating these practices is to establish a daily routine that includes time for self-care and healing rituals. Setting aside specific times of the day for meditation, visualizations, skin care and relaxation practices can help create a structure that supports skin health. Consistency is key, and repeating these practices over time amplifies their beneficial effects.

Practicing daily meditation is a powerful way to reduce stress, balance emotions and promote skin health. Guided meditations, focused on healing and visualizations, can be particularly effective. Find a quiet space, sit comfortably and close your eyes. Focus on your breathing, allowing each inhale and exhale to calm your mind and body. Visualize the healing light enveloping and permeating the skin, bringing regeneration and balance.

Incorporating the practice of grounding into your daily routine is another effective way to maintain skin health. Connecting directly with the earth helps to balance the body's energies and release accumulated stress. Spend time outdoors, walk barefoot on grass or sand, or simply sit in a park, allowing the energy of the earth to flow through you. This simple practice can have a significant impact on general well-being and skin health.

Self-care rituals, such as herbal baths, facial massages and the use of essential oils, should be incorporated on a regular basis. Baths with herbs such as chamomile, calendula and lavender not only help you relax, but also provide direct benefits for the skin. Prepare a warm bath, add herbal infusions and soak, visualizing the water as a healing agent that cleanses and revitalizes the skin. After bathing, apply essential oils in gentle massages, focusing on the areas that need the most care.

Keeping a self-care diary can be a useful tool for monitoring progress and adjusting practices as necessary. Writing down daily practices, foods consumed and changes observed in the skin can help identify patterns and make beneficial adjustments. This diary also serves as a constant reminder of dedication to self-care and well-being.

Integrating gratitude practices and positive affirmations into your daily routine can transform the way you view and care for your skin. Start and end the day by reflecting on the things you are grateful for and positively affirm the health and regeneration of your skin. Saying out loud or writing affirmations such as "My skin is healthy and radiant" or "I am grateful for my body's ability to heal" can create a positive mindset that supports healing.

Connecting with the community is also vital. Participating in healing circles, shamanic workshops and support groups can provide a sense of belonging and emotional support. Sharing experiences and practices with others who are on the same healing journey can offer new insights and strengthen the resolve to maintain daily practices. The sense of community and mutual support can be a powerful catalyst for healing.

Regular physical activity, such as yoga, tai chi or walking, is equally important. Physical exercise not only improves circulation and promotes detoxification, but also reduces stress and improves mood. Choose activities that are enjoyable and can be easily integrated into your daily routine.

Maintaining a balanced diet, rich in essential nutrients for skin health, is fundamental. Plan meals that include a variety of fruits, vegetables, whole grains, lean proteins and healthy fats. Avoid processed foods, refined sugars and trans fats, which can aggravate skin problems. Consciously preparing meals with intention and gratitude can turn eating into a self-care ritual.

Finally, it's important to be patient and gentle with yourself during the healing journey. Regenerating the skin and establishing a holistic lifestyle can take time, and every small step is progress. Celebrate the small victories and continue to dedicate yourself to practices that promote health and well-being.

By integrating these practices and rituals into a holistic lifestyle, it is possible not only to achieve healthy, radiant skin, but also to promote a harmonious balance between body, mind and spirit. This integral approach creates a solid foundation for overall well-being, providing a fuller and more conscious life.

Chapter 11
Immunity problems

Immunity is the body's ability to resist infection and disease. The immune system plays a crucial role in maintaining health, acting as a barrier against pathogenic microorganisms, toxins and cancer cells. However, various factors can compromise the efficiency of this system, leading to low immunity and increased susceptibility to disease.

Identifying immunity problems usually begins with observing frequent symptoms of infections, such as colds, flu, ear infections, tonsillitis and skin infections. These signs indicate that the body is having trouble fighting off invading agents. In addition, wounds that take a long time to heal and a general feeling of tiredness can be indicative of a weakened immune system.

The causes of low immunity are varied and can include an inadequate diet, chronic stress, lack of sleep, exposure to environmental toxins, and a sedentary lifestyle. Diet plays a key role in immunity. Diets poor in essential nutrients such as vitamins A, C, E, and D, as well as minerals such as zinc and iron, can compromise immune function. It is therefore essential to maintain a balanced diet rich in fruit, vegetables, whole grains and lean proteins.

Chronic stress is one of the main enemies of immunity. Constant stress can lead to increased levels of cortisol, a hormone which, at high levels, can suppress the immune response. Stress management techniques such as meditation, yoga and breathing exercises are effective in reducing the negative effects of stress on the body.

Lack of sleep is also directly related to immunity. During sleep, the body carries out various repair and regeneration functions, including the production of cytokines, proteins that play a vital role in the immune response. Sleep deprivation can reduce the production of these cytokines and other essential elements of the immune system, such as antibodies.

Exposure to environmental toxins, such as pollution, household chemicals and pesticides, can negatively affect the immune system. These toxins can cause inflammation and damage immune cells, reducing the body's ability to fight infections. Adopting healthier lifestyle practices, such as using natural and organic products, can help reduce the toxic load on the body.

A sedentary lifestyle is another factor that can have a negative impact on immunity. Regular physical exercise is known to strengthen the immune system. Moderate exercise, such as walking, cycling and swimming, helps increase blood circulation, promoting the mobilization of immune cells throughout the body. In addition, regular physical activity helps reduce stress and improves sleep quality.

Adopting a healthy lifestyle, which includes a balanced diet, regular exercise, stress management techniques and quality sleep, is fundamental to strengthening the immune system. In addition, connecting with nature and practicing purification rituals can complement these actions, promoting holistic health and well-being. From this integrative approach, it is possible to strengthen immunity and reduce susceptibility to disease, promoting a healthier and more balanced life.

In addition to the practices mentioned above, shamanism offers a variety of techniques to strengthen immunity that go beyond conventional approaches. The shamanic journey is one such technique. During the journey, the shaman enters an altered state of consciousness to connect with the spirit world and seek guidance and cures for immunity problems. This practice can reveal insights into energetic or spiritual imbalances that may be contributing to low immunity.

The practice of smoking with sacred herbs, such as sage, cedar and rosemary, is another powerful technique for purifying a person's environment and aura. The smoke from these herbs is known for its antibacterial and antiviral properties, helping to create a clean and energetically balanced space. Regular smoking can help remove negative energies that may be affecting the immune system.

The use of crystals is common in shamanic practices to strengthen immunity. Crystals such as amethyst, green quartz and black tourmaline are known for their healing and protective properties. Amethyst, for example, helps promote calm and balance, while green quartz is associated with physical healing. Black tourmaline, on the other hand, is used to protect against negative energies. These crystals can be used in meditations, placed in strategic locations in the home or carried as personal amulets.

Rituals to connect with nature also play an important role in maintaining immunity. Regular contact with the earth, such as walking barefoot in the grass or gardening, helps to "ground" the body's energy, promoting a balanced energy flow. Forest bathing, where you spend time in forests or green areas, has shown significant benefits for immune health, reducing cortisol levels and increasing the activity of immune cells.

Shamanic nutrition emphasizes the consumption of natural, whole foods. Including herbs and medicinal plants in the diet can provide additional support for the immune system. Herbs such as echinacea, known for its immunomodulatory properties, and ginger, with its anti-inflammatory properties, can be incorporated into teas, infusions or culinary preparations.

In addition to physical and energetic approaches, shamanism also emphasizes the importance of emotional and spiritual health in immunity. Negative and unresolved emotions, such as anger, sadness and fear, can weaken the immune system. Emotional healing practices, such as regression therapy or working with ancestral spirits, can help release these repressed emotions and restore emotional balance.

The practice of meditation and visualization is key to strengthening immunity. Guided meditations that involve visualizing healing light filling the body can help activate the immune system on an energetic level. Visualizing a white or golden light entering from the top of the head and spreading throughout the body can promote the healing and revitalization of immune cells.

The importance of sleep for immunity cannot be underestimated. During sleep, the body carries out various repair and regeneration functions, including the production of cytokines, which are essential for the immune response. Creating a healthy sleep routine, avoiding stimulants such as caffeine and electronics before bed, and maintaining a quiet, dark sleep environment can significantly improve sleep quality and, consequently, immunity.

Regular physical exercise is another essential component for maintaining immunity. Activities such as walking, yoga and tai chi not only improve blood circulation, but also help to reduce stress and promote a state of relaxation. Moderate, regular exercise is preferable to intense exercise, which can actually temporarily suppress immune function.

To complement immune-boosting practices, it is essential to explore the role of emotions and mental state in immune health. Shamanism recognizes that emotional balance is fundamental to the health of the body. Negative emotions, such as anger, sadness and fear, can create energetic blockages that compromise the immune system. Therefore, emotional release techniques are crucial to maintaining immunity.

A powerful shamanic practice is the inner journey to identify and release repressed emotions. During this journey, the shaman guides the individual into a state of altered consciousness, allowing them to access deep memories and emotions that may be affecting their health. The process of recognizing and releasing these emotions is essential for restoring emotional balance and strengthening immunity.

Another important technique is the use of positive affirmations and mental reprogramming. Negative beliefs and thoughts can weaken the immune response. Positive affirmations, repeated regularly, can help reprogram the mind to a healthier state. Examples of affirmations include "I am healthy and strong" and "My body is capable of healing itself". These statements help to create a positive mindset and promote health.

Connecting with the community is another vital aspect of immunity in shamanism. Social support and a sense of belonging can improve the immune response. Participating in healing circles, where individuals share their experiences and receive mutual support, strengthens not only the spirit, but also the body. The feeling of being connected to a support network provides emotional comfort and reduces stress.

Gratitude rituals are simple but extremely effective practices for improving immunity. Gratitude has been shown to have positive effects on physical and emotional well-being. Taking a moment every day to reflect on life's blessings and express gratitude helps to maintain a positive mindset and reduce stress. The practice of writing in a gratitude journal can be incorporated into the daily routine to reinforce this practice.

In addition to emotional and mental techniques, energy purification is essential for maintaining strong immunity. The regular practice of energy baths, using herbs such as rosemary, rue and lavender, helps to cleanse the aura and remove negative energies. These baths can be done weekly to maintain energy balance.

The practice of grounding is another effective technique for strengthening immunity. Connecting with the earth, whether by walking barefoot in nature or sitting on the ground, helps to balance the body's energies and reduce stress. Grounding allows the body to release excess negative energy and absorb the revitalizing energy of the earth.

The use of essential oils is a complementary practice in shamanism to strengthen immunity. Oils such as eucalyptus, tea tree and lemon have antimicrobial and immunomodulatory properties. Inhaling these oils or using them in massages can help protect the body against infections and strengthen the immune system.

Protective amulets are used in shamanism as a way of strengthening immunity. These amulets can be made of crystals, herbs or other natural elements and charged with intentions of health and protection. Wearing or carrying these amulets on a daily basis serves as a constant reminder of protection and well-being.

The practice of seasonal rituals is also significant in strengthening immunity. Celebrating the cycles of nature, such as solstices and equinoxes, helps to align the body with the natural rhythms of the world. These rituals can include the creation of seasonal altars, offerings to nature and meditations specific to each season. Harmony with natural cycles promotes a state of balance and strengthens the immune response.

To deepen the understanding and practice of immunity in shamanism, it is important to explore how specific spiritual practices and rituals can be integrated into everyday life to maintain and strengthen immunity.

One of the central practices is the creation and maintenance of a personal altar. The altar serves as a sacred space for meditation, prayer and daily rituals. It can be made up of elements that symbolize health and protection, such as crystals, herbs, candles and images of guardian spirits or power animals. Dedicating a few minutes every day to connecting with this space can help strengthen immunity by providing a moment of pause and spiritual reconnection.

Full moon and new moon rituals are powerful times to work on immunity. The full moon is an ideal time for purification and the release of energies that no longer serve, while the new moon is a good time to plant new intentions and healing energies. During the full moon, you can perform a cleansing ritual using salt water, purifying herbs and meditation. On the new moon, a ritual of planting intentions with crystals and specific herbs can help strengthen immunity for the next lunar cycle.

Contact with the natural elements is another fundamental practice. Each element - earth, water, fire and air - has healing qualities that can be integrated into daily practices. Walking barefoot on the earth (grounding) helps to stabilize and balance the body's energies. Water can be used in ritual baths with herbs, helping to energetically cleanse and revitalize. Fire, represented by candles or bonfires, can be used in purification and transformation rituals. Air, through conscious breathing and the use of incense, can bring mental clarity and spiritual purification.

Shamanic chants and mantras are powerful tools for strengthening immunity. Chanting or reciting specific mantras helps to raise the body's vibration and align energies. Mantras such as "I am protected" or "My immunity is strong" can be repeated daily to reinforce the intention of health. These chants can be incorporated into meditations or while carrying out daily tasks.

The practice of gratitude remains an essential tool. Gratitude not only improves emotional well-being, but also has proven effects on physical health. Taking a moment at the beginning and end of the day to reflect on the things you are grateful for helps maintain a positive outlook and reduce stress, thus strengthening immunity.

The use of amulets and talismans is an ancient tradition in shamanism for protection and strengthening immunity. Amulets made of crystals, such as amethyst and green quartz, or of herbs, such as rue and rosemary, can be carried with you or placed in strategic places in the house. These amulets are carried with intentions of health and protection, serving as a constant reminder of the healing work being done.

The practice of conscious breathing and guided meditation is crucial to keeping immunity high. Deep, controlled breathing helps to reduce stress and promote a state of calm. Guided meditations involving the visualization of healing light and the intention to strengthen immunity can be performed daily. Visualizing a golden or white light filling every cell of the body with health and vitality helps to align the mind and body with the intention of healing.

Connecting with ancestors and spirit guides is an integral part of shamanic practice. Asking the ancestors for guidance and protection through specific prayers and rituals can strengthen the sense of security and spiritual support. This connection can be cultivated through the creation of an ancestral altar, offerings and regular communications, such as meditations or night rituals.

To complete our approach to immunity in shamanism, we will explore some advanced techniques and daily practices that can be incorporated to maintain and strengthen the immune system on an ongoing basis.

One advanced practice in shamanism is working with power plants. These are plants that have significant medicinal and spiritual properties, such as ayahuasca, tobacco and peyote. However, it is important to approach these plants with great respect and under the guidance of an experienced shaman, as they have profound effects on the body and mind. These plants are used in ceremonies for deep cleansing, emotional and spiritual healing, and strengthening immunity.

Another advanced technique is voice healing, or toning. This practice involves using your own voice to emit sounds and vibrations that promote healing. Singing or chanting specific sounds can help align the body's energies and strengthen the immune system. Each sound or tone has a frequency that can influence different parts of the body and energy systems. Practicing toning regularly can help keep the body in a state of balance and health.

Practicing shamanic retreats is a powerful way to revitalize the immune system. Participating in a retreat, which can include shamanic journeys, healing ceremonies, meditations and deep connections with nature, provides a total immersion in healing practices. These retreats allow for a physical, emotional and spiritual detox, promoting a reset of the immune system and a general strengthening of health.

The energy scan technique is another useful practice. During the scan, the shaman uses their hands to feel and identify energy blockages or imbalances in the body. These blockages can be areas where energy is stagnant or flows improperly, compromising immunity. Once identified, the shaman uses various techniques to remove these blockages, such as the laying on of hands, the use of crystals or the channeling of healing energy.

The practice of energetic exercises, such as qigong or tai chi, is highly recommended to strengthen immunity. These exercises involve gentle movements and controlled breathing, promoting the harmonious flow of energy through the body. As well as improving immunity, these exercises help to reduce stress, increase flexibility and improve concentration.

Conscious eating remains an essential pillar for immunity. In shamanism, the preparation and consumption of food are seen as sacred acts. Preparing meals with intention and gratitude can raise the vibration of food, making it more nutritious and beneficial. Incorporating superfoods such as spirulina, chlorella, and medicinal mushrooms such as reishi and cordyceps can provide additional support for the immune system.

The practice of sound baths, or sound healing, uses instruments such as Tibetan bowls, gongs and bells to create sound vibrations that promote healing. These sounds can help balance the chakras, release tension and energy blockages and strengthen the immune system. Participating in sound bath sessions or incorporating these instruments into personal practices can be extremely beneficial.

Creating healing mandalas is another powerful technique. Mandalas are geometric designs that represent the wholeness and harmony of the universe. Creating and meditating with mandalas can help center the mind, promote calm and strengthen immunity. Mandalas can be hand-drawn, painted or made with natural elements such as flowers, stones and seeds.

Finally, the practice of offering and receiving blessings is fundamental. In shamanism, the exchange of positive energy is seen as a way of maintaining the flow of vital energy. Offering blessings to other people, to nature or to spirits, and being open to receiving blessings, creates a cycle of positive energy that strengthens immunity. Small daily gestures of kindness, gratitude and compassion have a profound impact on emotional and physical health.

In summary, strengthening immunity through shamanism involves a holistic approach that integrates physical, emotional, mental and spiritual practices. Using advanced techniques such as power plants, voice healing, shamanic retreats, energy scanning, energy exercises, conscious eating, sound baths, healing mandalas and the exchange of blessings, it is possible to maintain a robust and resilient immune system. These practices not only help prevent illness, but also promote a general state of well-being and balance, allowing the individual to live a full and healthy life. By incorporating these practices into daily life, it is possible to create a solid foundation for health and immunity, promoting a long and vibrant life.

Chapter 12
Self-esteem Problems

Self-esteem is a fundamental component of mental and emotional health. It influences how we see ourselves, how we relate to others and how we face life's challenges. Low self-esteem can manifest itself in various ways, including insecurity, feelings of inadequacy, fear of rejection and difficulty accepting praise or success. Identifying and understanding these signs is crucial to starting an effective healing process.

Low self-esteem often stems from past negative experiences. These experiences can include constant criticism in childhood, bullying, repeated failures or even emotional and physical trauma. These experiences can lead to a distorted view of oneself, where positive qualities are minimized and negative ones are exaggerated. In addition, constant comparison with others, especially on social media, can intensify these feelings of inadequacy.

The impact of low self-esteem on personal relationships is significant. People with low self-esteem can find it difficult to establish and maintain healthy relationships. They may feel unworthy of love and respect, which can lead to self-sabotaging behaviors such as social isolation or emotional dependency. These dynamics can create a vicious cycle, where a lack of self-confidence leads to negative social interactions, which in turn reinforce low self-esteem.

In the context of shamanism, healing low self-esteem involves a holistic approach that considers the individual in their entirety - body, mind and spirit. The first step in this process is to identify the negative thought patterns and limiting beliefs that sustain low self-esteem. This can be done through practices such as meditation, which help to bring these unconscious beliefs to the surface, allowing them to be recognized and transformed.

The shamanic journey is a powerful tool in this process of self-discovery and healing. During the journey, the practitioner enters an altered state of consciousness to connect with their spirit guides and gain insights into the origin of their low self-esteem. These guides can offer guidance and healing messages that help restructure the individual's self-perception, promoting a healthier and more positive sense of self.

The creation of a sacred space is essential for these healing practices. This space should be a safe and peaceful environment where the individual feels comfortable exploring their emotions and thoughts. Elements such as crystals, incense and spiritual symbols can be used to raise the energy of the environment and facilitate the spiritual connection. Purifying the space by burning sacred herbs, such as sage or palo santo, can help cleanse negative energies and promote an atmosphere of peace and introspection.

In addition, the use of positive affirmations is an effective technique for reprogramming the mind. Affirmations are phrases that reinforce a positive view of yourself, such as "I am worthy of love and respect" or "I am capable of overcoming any challenge". Repeating these affirmations daily can help replace negative thoughts with empowering beliefs, contributing to the development of a healthier self-esteem.

Another important aspect of healing low self-esteem is practicing gratitude. Taking daily moments to reflect on the positive aspects of life and recognize your own qualities and achievements can transform your perspective and increase your sense of self-worth. Keeping a gratitude journal, where you write down the things you are grateful for, can be a powerful tool in this process.

Integrating these practices into the daily routine can create a continuous state of balance and well-being, promoting the healing of low self-esteem and strengthening self-confidence. The healing journey is personal and unique, and each practice adopted contributes to a fuller state of health and a more balanced and harmonious life.

When delving into the process of healing low self-esteem, it is essential to consider the role of interpersonal relationships and how they influence our self-perception. Healthy relationships can reinforce self-esteem, while toxic relationships can undermine it. Therefore, part of the healing process involves an evaluation and possibly a redefinition of social interactions.

An effective technique in this respect is practicing healthy boundaries. Setting clear boundaries and respecting them is crucial to protecting one's energy and emotional well-being. This can include saying "no" to requests that drain energy, moving away from people who constantly criticize or disrespect, and seeking relationships that are mutually respectful and supportive. Setting boundaries not only protects the individual, but also sends a powerful message to the subconscious that they are worthy of respect and protection.

Practicing self-care is another important tool in building self-esteem. Self-care goes beyond occasional activities and involves an ongoing, holistic approach to nourishing the body, mind and spirit. This can include regular physical exercise, a balanced diet, adequate sleep, and activities that promote emotional well-being, such as hobbies, reading, or simply spending time in nature. Practicing self-care reinforces the message that you value yourself and deserve attention and care.

In shamanism, healing rituals are central to the process of regaining self-esteem. These rituals can include purification ceremonies, where sacred herbs are used to cleanse negative energies and renew vital energy. The creation of sand or stone mandalas, altars dedicated to spirit guides, and gratitude ceremonies are examples of practices that can help strengthen the spiritual connection and promote inner healing.

Shamanic journeying remains a powerful tool for exploring the roots of low self-esteem. During these journeys, the individual can meet and communicate with their spirit guides, who offer guidance and support. These spirit guides can help identify specific events or thought patterns that have contributed to low self-esteem and offer ways to overcome these challenges. Regularly connecting with these guides through meditation or rituals can provide an ongoing source of strength and guidance.

The practice of visualizations is an additional technique that can be integrated into the healing process. Positive visualizations help to reprogram the mind and create a new internal narrative. For example, visualizing yourself achieving goals, receiving love and respect, or living in harmony can help replace negative mental images with positive ones. These visualizations can be done during guided meditations or as part of a daily ritual.

The use of crystals in shamanism is also common to treat self-esteem issues. Crystals such as rose quartz, citrine and amethyst are known for their healing properties and can be used to promote self-love, confidence and mental clarity. These crystals can be carried with the intention of healing and kept close during meditations or placed on altars to strengthen their healing properties.

Another vital aspect of healing low self-esteem is the practice of forgiveness, both for oneself and for others. Holding on to resentment and blame can keep a person stuck in feelings of inadequacy and low self-esteem. Working on forgiveness, even gradually, can release these negative emotions and allow a sense of freedom and renewal. Forgiveness is not about forgetting or justifying harmful actions, but about releasing the power these memories have over emotional well-being.

Community and social support play an important role in building self-esteem. Participating in support groups, healing circles, or spiritual communities can provide a sense of belonging and validation. Sharing experiences with others who are on similar journeys can offer new perspectives and reinforce the feeling of not being alone.

Ultimately, the self-esteem healing journey is ongoing and requires patience and compassion with oneself. Every small step towards self-acceptance and self-love is significant. Recognizing and celebrating this progress, no matter how small, can help maintain motivation and keep moving forward on the path to healing. Integrating these practices into daily life can profoundly transform self-perception, promoting healthy and sustainable self-esteem.

When moving forward on the journey of healing low self-esteem, it is important to recognize the interconnection between the mind, body and spirit. Practices that integrate these three aspects can provide deeper and longer-lasting healing. The integration of physical, emotional and spiritual techniques allows for a comprehensive approach to rebuilding self-esteem.

One physical practice that can help heal self-esteem is dance. Dancing, especially in a ritualistic or spiritual context, can release emotional and energetic blockages, promoting a sense of freedom and personal expression. Moving the body to the sound of drums or music can help release accumulated tensions and reconnect with one's inner strength. The act of dancing can be a powerful way of expressing emotions and affirming one's identity and value.

The practice of yoga can also be incorporated to strengthen self-esteem. Yoga not only improves physical strength and flexibility, but also promotes mental calm and spiritual clarity. Heart-opening yoga poses, such as warrior pose and cobra pose, can help open the heart center, promoting feelings of self-love and acceptance. Regular yoga practice can create a deeper connection with one's body, helping to cultivate a positive body image and a sense of well-being.

Nutrition is another fundamental aspect of healing self-esteem. A balanced and nutritious diet can significantly influence mood and energy. Foods rich in essential vitamins and minerals, such as fruit, vegetables, nuts and seeds, can support mental and emotional health. Avoiding processed and sugar-rich foods can prevent mood swings and promote a more stable mental state. The act of preparing and consuming healthy meals can be seen as an act of self-care, reinforcing the message that you value yourself.

Journaling or therapeutic writing is an effective tool for exploring and transforming thoughts and feelings related to self-esteem. Keeping a journal can provide a safe space to express emotions, reflect on experiences and identify negative thought patterns. Writing about one's feelings in an honest and non-judgmental way can help to clear the mind and process difficult emotions. In addition, writing can be used to set goals and affirm positive intentions, contributing to the construction of a more empowering internal narrative.

In the context of shamanism, connecting with nature is a central practice for healing self-esteem. Spending time in natural environments can help restore energy balance and promote a sense of belonging and connection. Activities such as walking in the forest, meditating by a river or simply sitting in a park can provide a space for introspection and spiritual renewal. Nature has an intrinsic healing power that can help relieve stress and anxiety, allowing self-esteem to flourish.

Practicing gratitude rituals in nature can strengthen this connection. For example, when hiking, you can take small gifts, such as flowers or stones, to offer to the earth as a form of gratitude. This act of giving and receiving with nature can create a sense of reciprocity and respect, reinforcing self-worth and interconnectedness with the world around you.

In addition, practicing conscious breathing techniques in natural environments can amplify their benefits. Breathing deeply of fresh, clean air while surrounded by natural beauty can help calm the mind and align the body's energy. Techniques such as 4-7-8 breathing or alternate breathing can be practiced outdoors to promote a state of peace and mental clarity.

In shamanism, the creation of talismans or personal amulets can be a meaningful practice to strengthen self-esteem. These sacred objects can be charged with specific intentions and used as physical reminders of inner worth and strength. Talismans can be made from natural materials, such as stones, shells, feathers or wood, and can be consecrated through rituals and ceremonies. Carrying a talisman or amulet can provide a sense of protection and empowerment, reinforcing self-esteem on a daily basis.

The integration of these holistic and spiritual practices can profoundly transform self-perception, promoting healthy and lasting self-esteem. Healing self-esteem is an ongoing and personal process, and each step taken towards self-love and self-acceptance contributes to a more balanced and harmonious life.

As you continue to explore practices that help build and strengthen self-esteem, it is essential to consider the power of affirmations and positive thinking. The mind is a powerful tool and can be trained to focus on the positive, promoting a healthier view of oneself.

Positive affirmations are statements that reinforce a positive and empowering image of yourself. Repeating affirmations daily can help reprogram the mind, replacing negative, self-critical thoughts with positive, uplifting beliefs. Some effective affirmations include "I am worthy of love and respect," "I trust in myself and my abilities," and "I am enough just as I am." These affirmations can be repeated out loud, written in a journal, or placed in visible places, such as mirrors or work desks, to serve as constant reminders.

The practice of mindfulness meditation is another powerful technique for improving self-esteem. Mindfulness involves being present in the moment and accepting your thoughts and feelings without judgment. This practice helps you develop an attitude of acceptance and compassion for yourself, recognizing that all human beings have flaws and imperfections. Guided meditations focused on self-compassion can be particularly useful. These meditations encourage you to send love and kindness to yourself, promoting a sense of inner peace and acceptance.

In addition, cultivating self-compassion is vital for healing self-esteem. Self-compassion involves treating yourself with the same kindness and understanding that you would offer a close friend. It means acknowledging one's own mistakes and shortcomings without harsh judgment, understanding that they are part of the human experience. Self-compassion practices can include developing a kinder internal dialog, where you talk to yourself in an encouraging and understanding way, and practicing exercises that reinforce your own kindness, such as the "butterfly hug," where you cross your arms over your chest and give yourself a hug.

Healing through art is another effective approach to strengthening self-esteem. Artistic activities, such as painting, drawing, creative writing, or playing a musical instrument, allow for the free expression of emotions and thoughts. Art can be a therapeutic way of processing experiences and connecting with one's own creativity and authenticity. Taking part in artistic workshops or simply setting aside regular time for creative activities can be a powerful way of nurturing self-esteem and celebrating individuality.

In the context of shamanism, healing rituals involving elements of nature can provide a deep reconnection with one's essence. Building sand or stone mandalas, creating altars with natural elements, and practicing purification ceremonies with water are all examples of how nature can be integrated into healing practice. These rituals not only promote physical and emotional healing, but also reinforce the spiritual connection, reminding the individual of their interconnectedness with the universe.

The practice of gratitude continues to be a fundamental tool in strengthening self-esteem. Gratitude helps to focus the mind on the positive, celebrating one's own qualities and achievements, as well as daily blessings. Keeping a gratitude journal, where you regularly record things you are grateful for, can help cultivate a mindset of abundance and appreciation. In addition, expressing gratitude to others, whether through words or actions, can strengthen relationships and foster a sense of community and support.

Integrating grounding exercises can help strengthen self-esteem by promoting a sense of stability and security. Grounding exercises involve techniques that help connect with the present and stabilize the body's energy. This can include walking barefoot in the grass, sitting by a tree, or simply breathing deeply and feeling the contact between your feet and the ground. These practices help to anchor the energy, reducing anxiety and promoting a sense of rootedness and security.

Participating in healing circles or support groups can provide a safe and supportive environment for exploring and healing self-esteem. These groups offer a space where one can share experiences, receive support and learn from the journey of others. The sense of belonging and community that arises from these circles can bolster confidence and self-esteem, reminding you that you are not alone in your healing journey.

When addressing the issue of self-esteem, it is vital to explore the importance of acceptance and authenticity. Being authentic, i.e. living according to one's own values and desires, rather than trying to conform to the expectations of others, is fundamental to healthy self-esteem. Authenticity involves accepting yourself fully, with all your flaws and imperfections, and allowing your true essence to show through.

Acceptance begins with recognizing that everyone has imperfections and that perfection is not a realistic or necessary goal in order to be worthy of love and respect. This concept is central to shamanism, which sees each individual as a complete and valuable being exactly as they are. Self-knowledge practices, such as reflection and meditation, can help identify and embrace these imperfections, allowing for a deeper acceptance of oneself.

The practice of authenticity can be cultivated in various ways. First, it's important to identify your own values and desires. This can be done through reflection exercises, such as writing a personal manifesto or creating a list of priority values. Understanding what is truly important allows you to live according to these principles, which strengthens self-esteem and promotes a more satisfying life.

Authentic communication is another essential aspect. Expressing thoughts and feelings honestly and respectfully, even when it's difficult, helps to build relationships based on trust and mutual respect. In shamanism, communication is often seen as a bridge between the inner and outer worlds, and being honest with oneself and others is fundamental to integrity and spiritual well-being.

The practice of service and contribution can also strengthen self-esteem. Helping others and contributing to the well-being of the community can create a sense of purpose and personal value. In shamanism, service to others is seen as an expression of connection and reciprocity with the world. Participating in community activities, volunteering or simply helping friends and family can promote feelings of usefulness and connection.

Energy healing is a common practice in shamanism that can be used to balance personal energy and promote self-esteem. Techniques such as the laying on of hands, the use of healing crystals and the practice of reiki can help to clear energy blockages and restore the natural flow of vital energy. Regular energy healing sessions can provide ongoing support for emotional and spiritual health.

Another effective practice is the use of empowering visualizations. During meditation, visualizing yourself achieving goals, overcoming challenges and living by your own values can boost confidence and self-esteem. These visualizations can be done daily and combined with positive affirmations to maximize their effects. Visualizing a bright light or a personal symbol of power, such as a power animal or spiritual guide, can serve as an anchor of strength and confidence.

Practicing self-honoring rituals can be a powerful way to strengthen self-esteem. These rituals can include celebrating small victories and achievements, creating personal altars with symbols of success and growth, and holding ceremonies of gratitude and personal recognition. Honoring oneself and one's efforts sends a clear message to the subconscious that one is valuable and worthy of recognition.

The role of spirit guides and power animals in shamanism is also fundamental to healing self-esteem. These spiritual beings offer protection, wisdom and support, helping to guide the individual on their journey of self-discovery and healing. Maintaining a regular connection with these guides through meditation, shamanic journeys and rituals can provide a sense of security and guidance, strengthening inner confidence.

Attending spiritual retreats or personal development workshops can provide a safe space to explore and strengthen self-esteem. These events offer the opportunity to learn new healing techniques, share experiences with others and receive support from experienced facilitators. Immersion in an environment dedicated to personal and spiritual growth can catalyze deep and lasting change.

Finally, the continuous practice of self-care is essential for maintaining self-esteem. This includes taking care of the body through a balanced diet and regular exercise, nourishing the mind with inspiring reading and continuous learning, and feeding the spirit through regular spiritual practices and meaningful connections. Integrating these practices into daily life helps to create a solid foundation of self-love and well-being.

The journey to strengthening self-esteem is personal and unique, and each practice adopted contributes to a deeper state of self-confidence and acceptance. With patience, dedication and the integration of these practices, it is possible to transform self-perception and live a fuller, more balanced and authentically satisfying life.

Chapter 13
Fears and Phobias

Fears and phobias are intense and irrational responses to certain stimuli or situations, triggered by a variety of factors, from traumatic experiences to genetic predispositions. While fear is a natural and adaptive response to real danger, phobias are exacerbated fears that interfere with everyday life, often without a real threat present. In the shamanic context, fears and phobias are seen as energetic blockages that can arise from past traumas, loss of soul parts, or negative spiritual influences. These blockages prevent the natural flow of vital energy through the body, resulting in feelings of anxiety and panic.

The physical and emotional symptoms associated with fears and phobias are varied and can include heart palpitations, excessive sweating, trembling, feeling faint or dizzy, nausea, a sense of dread or extreme terror and an intense desire to flee from the feared situation or object. In addition to these physical symptoms, fears and phobias can lead to social isolation, damage to professional and personal life, and a significantly reduced quality of life. The person may avoid situations that trigger fear, limiting their activities and opportunities for growth.

The impact of fears and phobias on daily life can be profound. People with specific phobias can drastically alter their routines to avoid the feared object or situation. For example, someone with a phobia of flying may avoid air travel, limiting professional and personal opportunities. Generalized fears, such as social anxiety, can lead to difficulties in forming and maintaining relationships, impacting emotional health and well-being. These exacerbated fear responses can result in a vicious cycle of avoidance and increased anxiety. The inability to face and overcome these fears can lead to a sense of helplessness and hopelessness, further exacerbating anxiety symptoms.

The causes of fears and phobias can be complex and multifaceted. Among the most common are traumatic experiences, genetic predisposition and learned conditioning. Past painful or traumatic events can leave a deep mark, resulting in irrational fears associated with stimuli related to the trauma. Genetics can play a role in predisposition to phobias, with some individuals more prone to developing these conditions. In addition, observing and learning fears from family members or other authority figures can influence the development of phobias.

To address and heal fears and phobias through shamanic practices, it is crucial to prepare the environment and the individual properly. Preparation involves creating a safe and sacred space where energy can flow freely and healing intentions can be set. Common elements used include crystals, candles, medicinal plants and spiritual symbols that help to create a protective and healing environment. Choosing a quiet time and a place where the practitioner feels safe and will not be interrupted, preferably a space dedicated to meditation and spiritual practices, is essential.

Creating a sacred space helps to focus the practitioner's mind and energy, facilitating the connection with spiritual guides and promoting an environment conducive to healing. With proper preparation, the ritual can be conducted more effectively, helping to release fears and restore emotional balance.

The shamanic approach to treating fears and phobias begins with identifying the emotional and spiritual roots of these feelings. Often, fears and phobias are associated with past traumas that result in fragmentation of the soul, where parts of the individual's essence separate as a form of protection. This process of losing parts of the soul can lead to a constant feeling of fear and vulnerability, as the individual doesn't feel complete. The shaman, acting as a mediator between the physical and spiritual worlds, works to locate and reintegrate these lost parts of the soul.

The process of recovering the soul is a central practice in shamanism. During a shamanic journey, the shaman enters an altered state of consciousness through the use of drums, rattles or entheogenic plants, and travels to the spirit world in search of the lost parts of the patient's soul. This journey is accompanied by spirit guides who offer protection and guidance. On finding these parts of the soul, the shaman brings them back to the physical world and reintegrates them into the individual, restoring their vital energy and promoting a sense of completeness and security.

In addition to recovering the soul, the shaman can use various purification techniques to release fears and phobias. Smoking with sacred herbs such as sage, cedar or palo santo is a common practice that helps to cleanse negative energies and create a healing environment. The smoke from these herbs is considered an offering to the spirits and a means of energy purification. During the ritual, the shaman can guide the patient to focus on the areas of their life where fear and phobia are most present, allowing the smoke to purify these areas and restore balance.

The shamanic journey can also include identifying and removing negative energies that contribute to fears and phobias. These energies can be negative spiritual entities or simply accumulations of stagnant energy in the individual's energy field. The shaman, through his practices and spiritual connections, identifies these energies and removes them, allowing the flow of vital energy to be restored.

Connecting with animal spirits or spirit guides is another powerful technique for treating fears and phobias. These guides offer protection, strength and wisdom, helping the individual to face and overcome their fears. During a shamanic journey, the patient can meet their animal spirit or spirit guide, receiving messages and guidance that help them deal with their fears more effectively. The presence of these guides can offer a sense of security and support, which is fundamental to the healing process.

The use of crystals is another common practice in shamanic healing. Crystals such as amethyst, which promotes calm and peace, and obsidian, which offers protection and helps to release fears, can be used during rituals. These crystals are placed at specific points on the body or in the healing environment to amplify the healing energy and promote balance. The patient can be guided to carry these crystals with them or to place them in their sacred space as a constant reminder of protection and healing.

Throughout the healing process, it is important that the patient actively participates, setting clear intentions and being open to the healing experience. The shaman guides the patient through meditations and visualizations that help focus the mind and direct the healing energy to where it is most needed. These practices not only help to release fears and phobias, but also strengthen the patient's spiritual connection, promoting a lasting sense of peace and security.

The patient's mental and emotional preparation is crucial to the success of shamanic rituals designed to treat fears and phobias. The shaman works to create an environment of trust and safety, where the patient feels comfortable exploring and confronting their fears. Meditation and conscious breathing are essential practices that help calm the mind and body, allowing the patient to enter a receptive and relaxed state before the ritual. Deep breathing techniques, such as inhaling slowly through the nose and exhaling through the mouth, help to reduce anxiety and prepare the energy field for healing.

During the ritual, music and sounds play an important role in inducing altered states of consciousness. The rhythmic sound of the drum, for example, is used to facilitate the shamanic journey, helping the patient to disconnect from the distractions of the physical world and enter a deep meditative state. The steady beat of the drum creates a frequency that resonates with the brain waves, promoting a sense of calm and spiritual openness. Other instruments, such as rattles and flutes, can also be used to intensify the experience and direct the healing energy.

Visualization is a powerful tool in shamanic practice. The shaman guides the patient through visualizations that help identify and confront fears. For example, the patient can be guided to visualize a protective light around them, which dispels the shadows of fear and brings a sense of security. Visualizing facing the feared object or situation in a controlled and safe environment can help reduce the intensity of the fear response in real life. These visualizations are reinforced with positive affirmations that help reprogram the mind for calmer, more controlled responses.

Chants and mantras are also used to amplify the healing energy. Repeating specific words or phrases during the ritual helps to focus the mind and channel the healing intention. Chants are often passed down from generation to generation and have a deep spiritual meaning. They are used to invoke the presence of guiding spirits, protect sacred space and direct healing energy. The repetition of mantras creates a vibration that resonates with the patient's energy field, helping to release blockages and restore balance.

Integration is a vital aspect of the healing process. After the ritual, the patient is encouraged to reflect on the experience and write down any insights or messages received during the journey. This period of reflection is crucial for assimilating the energetic and emotional changes that have taken place. Regular practice of relaxation and meditation techniques at home helps to maintain the beneficial effects of the ritual and promote ongoing healing. Keeping a fear diary, where the patient can record their progress and challenges, can also be useful for monitoring the evolution of the healing process.

Shamanic healing rituals are not a one-size-fits-all solution, but part of an ongoing process of growth and self-discovery. Regular practice of these techniques, combined with the support of an experienced shaman, can lead to a significant reduction in fears and phobias over time. Reconnecting with one's spirituality and strengthening the link with one's spiritual guides is fundamental to maintaining emotional and energetic balance. By cultivating this spiritual connection, the patient can develop greater resilience and the ability to face future challenges with more confidence and serenity.

The use of natural elements, such as crystals and medicinal plants, continues to be an important practice in the healing process. Amethyst and rose quartz, for example, can be used to promote peace and emotional healing, while herbs such as chamomile and valerian help to calm the mind and body. These elements are integrated into the sacred space and used in daily rituals to maintain the energy of healing and protection. Practicing gratitude and making offerings to the guiding spirits are also effective ways of maintaining harmony and spiritual connection.

Continuing the healing process involves incorporating daily practices that support the release of fears and phobias. An essential element is the practice of grounding, which helps maintain the connection with the earth and the energy present. Walking barefoot in nature, sitting by a tree or simply touching the earth with your hands are effective ways of releasing accumulated negative energy and re-establishing balance. Direct contact with nature provides a sense of stability and security, which are fundamental for dealing with fears.

In addition to grounding, practicing conscious breathing throughout the day can help regulate emotional responses and reduce anxiety. Breathing exercises such as 4-7-8 breathing, where you breathe in for four seconds, hold your breath for seven seconds and breathe out slowly for eight seconds, are especially useful. This technique activates the parasympathetic nervous system, promoting a state of deep relaxation. Integrating these exercises at times of stress or before bed can make a significant difference in managing fears and phobias.

Creating a supportive sleep environment is crucial, as a good night's sleep strengthens emotional resilience. Keeping the bedroom dark, quiet and cool, free from electronic devices, helps prepare the body and mind for rest. Using diffusers with essential oils such as lavender or chamomile can promote a relaxing environment and make it easier to fall asleep. In addition, practicing evening rituals, such as taking a hot bath with Epsom salts or practicing guided meditation, signals to the body that it's time to rest, helping to reduce anxiety and prepare for restful sleep.

Diet also plays an important role in managing fears and phobias. Foods rich in tryptophan, such as nuts, seeds and bananas, help in the production of serotonin, which regulates mood and promotes a sense of well-being. Avoiding stimulants such as caffeine and refined sugar, especially in the evening, can help maintain a state of calm and balance. Staying hydrated and consuming a balanced diet rich in nutrients supports the body and mind, providing the energy needed to face emotional challenges.

Gratitude rituals are a powerful practice for transforming the mindset and reducing fear. Taking a few minutes every day to reflect on the things you are grateful for helps refocus the mind on positive aspects of life, reducing the tendency to focus on fears. Keeping a gratitude journal, where you write down three things you are grateful for each day, can create a mental state of contentment and peace. This simple but effective practice helps to reduce stress and promote a more balanced and positive outlook.

The ongoing connection with spirit guides and power animals is strengthened through regular meditation and prayer practices. Spirit guides offer protection, wisdom and support, helping the individual to face fears with more confidence. During meditations, visualizing these guides by your side, offering guidance and protection, can reinforce the feeling of security. Making regular offerings, such as flowers, food or other symbolic items, shows gratitude and keeps the spiritual connection strong.

Healing circles and support groups also play a vital role in the healing process. Attending regular meetings with others who are facing similar challenges can provide a sense of community and emotional support. Sharing experiences, practices and insights in a safe and welcoming environment helps to strengthen resilience and promote healing. The exchange of wisdom and healing techniques between group members offers new ways of facing and overcoming fears.

Artistic practice as a form of emotional expression is another effective tool. Activities such as painting, writing, dance or music allow emotions to be expressed in a safe and creative way. Art not only provides a means of emotional release, but also helps to better process and understand fears. Integrating artistic activities into your daily or weekly routine can be a powerful way of maintaining emotional balance and reducing anxiety.

Maintaining a balanced lifestyle that includes regular physical exercise, adequate rest and time for relaxation is essential. The shaman can offer guidance on which practices and routines are most suitable for each individual, taking into account their specific needs and the nature of their fears. Exercises such as yoga, tai chi or walks in nature are especially effective for promoting calm and well-being.

The practice of visualization remains an essential tool in the treatment of fears and phobias. Daily visualizations of a safe and peaceful place can help establish a mental state of peace and security. For example, the patient can imagine themselves in a serene forest, where every detail - the sound of the leaves, the singing of birds, the gentle breeze - contributes to a feeling of comfort and protection. This regular practice not only helps to reduce anxiety, but also strengthens the ability to face feared situations with more confidence.

In addition to visualizations, incorporating mantras and positive affirmations can have a significant impact on reducing fears. Repeating phrases such as "I am brave", "I am safe" or "I am able to face my fears" reinforces the subconscious mind with messages of strength and security. These affirmations can be recited during meditation, when waking up or before going to sleep, creating a solid foundation of self-confidence that permeates everyday life.

The practice of self-compassion is vital in the healing process. Often, individuals struggling with fears and phobias feel guilty or ashamed of their reactions. Learning to treat yourself with kindness and understanding, recognizing that fears are natural responses and that it takes time to overcome them, is crucial. The shaman can guide the patient in self-compassion practices, helping them to develop a more loving and patient attitude towards themselves.

Release rituals are another powerful technique for dealing with fears and phobias. These rituals involve symbolically releasing the fear by writing it down on a piece of paper and then burning it in a fire or with a candle. This physical action of releasing fear can be extremely cathartic, helping the patient to leave behind negative emotions and make room for feelings of courage and peace. Performing this ritual during the full moon, a traditional time of release and renewal, can amplify its effects.

Integrating spiritual practices into the daily routine helps maintain energetic and emotional balance. Setting aside time each day to connect with one's spirituality, whether through meditation, prayer or reading sacred texts, strengthens the connection with the divine and provides a sense of peace and purpose. This regular practice helps to anchor the individual, providing a solid basis for facing and overcoming fears.

In addition, it is essential to create a support network, made up of friends, family or professionals who can offer emotional support and guidance. Joining support groups or healing circles, where you can share experiences and receive advice, can be extremely beneficial. Knowing that you are not alone in your fight against fears and phobias provides comfort and encouragement.

Practicing gratitude is a simple but effective technique for transforming your mindset and reducing your focus on fears. Taking a moment every day to reflect on the things you are grateful for helps to cultivate a positive attitude and reduce anxiety. Keeping a gratitude journal, where you write down three things you are grateful for each day, can create a mental state of contentment and peace, helping to shift the focus from fears to the positive aspects of life.

Regular physical exercise also plays a crucial role in managing fears and phobias. Activities such as yoga, tai chi, walking and swimming help to release endorphins, promoting a sense of well-being and reducing anxiety. In addition, regular physical exercise improves general health, providing more energy and emotional resilience. The shaman can recommend specific practices that align the body and mind, helping to maintain balance and reduce fears.

Finally, it is important for the patient to engage in activities that bring them joy and satisfaction. Hobbies, such as painting, gardening, reading or any other pleasurable activity, help to divert the mind from fears and focus on positive aspects of life. These activities not only provide an outlet for emotional expression, but also help to build a balanced and fulfilling life.

The path to overcoming fears and phobias is an ongoing process that requires dedication and regular practice. With the support of a shaman and the incorporation of spiritual, physical and emotional practices into the daily routine, it is possible to transform fears into strengths, promoting a life of peace and balance. Reconnecting with one's essence and creating a supportive and safe environment are fundamental to the success of this healing process.

Chapter 14
Relationship Problems

Relationship problems are issues that can profoundly affect an individual's quality of life. They manifest themselves in various ways, such as frequent conflicts, lack of communication, accumulated resentment and the inability to resolve differences constructively. These problems can arise in both personal and professional relationships, impacting on the emotional and mental health of the people involved. Identifying the symptoms of relationship problems is a crucial step in starting the healing process. Common signs include constant arguing, a sense of detachment, a lack of empathy, and the presence of persistent negative feelings such as anger and frustration. In addition, behaviors such as avoiding interaction or communication and a preference for spending time away from the partner are clear indicators that there is something wrong in the relational dynamic.

Understanding the underlying causes of relationship problems is essential to addressing them effectively. Lack of communication is one of the most common causes. When individuals don't express their thoughts and feelings clearly and openly, misunderstandings and conflicts can easily arise. Effective communication involves not only talking, but also listening carefully and validating the other person's feelings. Personal differences, such as values, beliefs and expectations, can also generate tension. These differences, when not managed properly, can lead to misunderstandings and resentment. Other causes include past experiences, such as traumas or dysfunctional relationship patterns learned in childhood, which can negatively influence the way individuals relate to each other.

The shamanic approach to treating relationship problems involves creating a sacred space where healing can take place. This space should be quiet and free of distractions, allowing for a deep connection with the spiritual world. Purifying the space by burning sacred herbs, such as sage or cedar, helps to cleanse negative energies and create an environment conducive to healing. A clear intention to heal the relationship must be established, forming a solid foundation for the ritual.

The materials needed for the ritual include drums or rattles to facilitate entering trance states, healing crystals such as rose quartz, which promotes love and understanding, and essential oils of lavender or ylang-ylang to induce relaxation and harmony. The shaman can prepare an altar with symbols that represent union and cooperation, such as shells, stones and feathers, to invoke the presence of the guardian spirits.

The ritual begins with a guided meditation, where the shaman takes the participants into a state of deep relaxation. Conscious, rhythmic breathing helps to stabilize the body and mind, facilitating the transition to an altered state of consciousness. During the shamanic journey, the shaman can meet and interact with spirit guides or power animals who offer wisdom and insights into the causes of relationship problems and the appropriate solutions.

During the shamanic journey, the shaman can use the rhythmic sound of the drum to facilitate communication with the spirit guides. These guides can offer insights into the nature of conflicts and the best ways to address them. An important aspect of this process is the identification of negative patterns of behavior and communication that perpetuate relationship problems. By bringing these patterns to consciousness, it is possible to start working on transforming them.

Shamanic healing for relationship problems can also involve practicing emotional release rituals. These rituals help to release accumulated negative feelings, such as anger, resentment and sadness, which may be blocking connection and harmony between individuals. Burning paper where participants write down their negative emotions can be a symbolic way of releasing these feelings. This practice helps to clear the energy field and make room for more positive and constructive emotions.

The integration of medicinal plants is a fundamental part of the healing process. Herbs such as chamomile and valerian can be used to promote calm and relaxation, helping participants to feel more balanced and receptive during the healing process. Teas from these herbs can be consumed before rituals or during moments of reflection to facilitate the release of tension and promote a state of inner peace.

Conscious communication is an essential skill that can be improved through shamanic practices. The shaman can guide participants in active listening and authentic expression exercises, teaching them to communicate their feelings and needs in a clear and respectful way. The practice of speaking and listening with an open heart can transform relationship dynamics, promoting deeper mutual understanding and reducing conflict.

Connecting with the elements of nature can also be a powerful source of healing for relationship problems. Spending time outdoors, in contact with the earth, water, air and fire, can help restore inner balance and strengthen the bond between individuals. Hiking in forests, meditating by rivers or lakes and practicing rituals around campfires are all effective ways of harnessing the healing energy of nature.

Creating a sacred space in the home, where healing rituals can be performed regularly, is another practice that can support the resolution of relationship problems. This space should be kept clean and energetically balanced, with the regular burning of sacred herbs for purification. Including elements of nature, such as plants, stones and water, can help create an atmosphere of serenity and connection.

The use of visualizations and guided meditations can help participants connect with the healing energy of spirit guides and the elements of nature. Visualizing a healing light surrounding you and your partner can help dissolve emotional barriers and promote harmony. These practices can be carried out daily, as part of a routine of self-care and strengthening the relationship.

The practice of gratitude is a powerful tool for transforming the energy of a relationship. Taking a moment every day to express gratitude for your partner's positive qualities and actions can help cultivate an attitude of appreciation and mutual respect. Keeping a gratitude journal where you write down these qualities can serve as a constant reminder of why the relationship is valuable.

The shamanic journey to resolve relationship problems is an ongoing process that involves dedication and regular practice. By integrating these techniques and practices into everyday life, it is possible to transform relationship dynamics, promoting healing, harmony and deep connection between individuals. This path not only relieves the symptoms of relationship problems, but also strengthens the foundation of the relationship, creating an environment where both partners can grow and thrive together.

The practice of forgiveness rituals is a powerful shamanic technique for resolving relationship problems. Forgiveness is a profound act that releases the person from accumulated resentments and hurts, allowing healing and reconciliation to take place. During a forgiveness ritual, participants are guided to reflect on the events that caused pain and to express their feelings honestly and openly. The visualization of a healing light surrounding both participants can facilitate the process of releasing resentments. This ritual can be performed regularly, helping to keep the relationship free of negative emotional charges.

In addition to forgiveness rituals, the practice of empathy exercises is fundamental. The shaman can guide participants to put themselves in the other person's shoes, understanding their feelings and perspectives. Exercises such as "empathic listening", where one person speaks while the other listens without interrupting, help to develop a deeper and more compassionate understanding. After listening, the person listening repeats what they have understood, validating the other's feelings and ensuring that both feel heard and understood.

Reconnecting with ancestral roots is another practice that can strengthen relationships. Shamanism values the wisdom of the ancestors and believes that they can offer guidance and support. Holding ceremonies to honor the ancestors, expressing gratitude and asking for wisdom, can help bring valuable insights into inherited relationship patterns and how to transform them. These ceremonies can include offerings of food, flowers and symbolic objects, creating a bridge between the present and the lessons of the past.

The regular practice of meditation in pairs is an effective way of strengthening the spiritual and emotional connection between partners. Sitting together in silence, focusing on the breath and the presence of the other, can create a space of intimacy and understanding. Guided meditation can include visualizations of light and healing energy flowing between partners, dissolving barriers and promoting harmony. This practice not only calms the mind, but also strengthens the energetic connection between individuals.

The use of symbolic objects in the relationship can serve as constant reminders of the intention to heal and connect. Creating amulets or talismans together, using elements from nature such as stones, shells and feathers, can be a symbolic act of union. These objects can be carried or placed in meaningful places, reinforcing the intention to maintain harmony and love in the relationship. The process of creating these objects can also be a bonding activity, promoting cooperation and creativity.

The practice of periodic renewal rituals is essential for maintaining the vitality of the relationship. These rituals can be carried out on special occasions, such as anniversaries or changes of season, and can include renewing vows or setting new intentions for the relationship. Creating a temporary altar with symbols of renewal, such as fresh flowers and candles, can help create a sacred atmosphere for the ritual. During the ritual, participants can share their hopes and wishes for the future, reinforcing the commitment to growth and mutual support.

Shamanic healing for relationship problems is not limited to the sacred space of the ritual. It's important to integrate the lessons and practices into everyday life. Practicing gratitude and appreciation every day, even for small actions, helps to maintain a positive and constructive attitude. Making time for joint activities that promote fun and connection, such as walks in nature, cooking together or practicing a shared hobby, strengthens the relationship.

Shamanic healing for relationship problems involves a holistic approach that considers the physical, emotional, mental and spiritual well-being of individuals. By integrating forgiveness rituals, empathy exercises, ancestral reconnection, meditation, the use of symbolic objects and renewal rituals into the relationship routine, it is possible to promote deep and lasting transformation. These practices not only resolve existing conflicts, but also strengthen the basis of the relationship, creating an environment of love, respect and cooperation where both partners can thrive together.

The importance of self-knowledge in the context of relationship problems cannot be underestimated. Shamanism emphasizes the need to know and understand oneself as a crucial step in resolving conflicts and strengthening connections with others. The shaman can guide participants on inner journeys to explore their own emotions, beliefs and behavior patterns. These introspective journeys help to identify and transform inner aspects that may be contributing to relationship problems.

Personal journaling is an effective tool for promoting self-knowledge. Writing regularly about feelings, experiences and reflections allows for a greater understanding of one's own thoughts and emotions. This habit can help identify negative patterns and develop strategies to address them constructively. The journal can also include records of dreams, insights received during meditations or rituals, and intentions for healing the relationship.

Family lineage healing rituals are another powerful practice in shamanism for addressing relationship problems. Often, current conflicts are rooted in past family patterns and traumas. The shaman can conduct rituals that involve invoking and healing ancestral lineages, releasing inherited negative patterns and promoting peace and harmony in the family. These rituals can include offerings, prayers and the visualization of healing for the ancestors, acknowledging and honouring their struggles and contributing to the transformation of these patterns.

Practicing emotional bonding rituals can help strengthen the connection between partners. These rituals can involve creating symbols of union, such as making a necklace or bracelet together using stones and natural elements that symbolize love and harmony. Performing these rituals at special times, such as anniversaries or significant dates, can reinforce mutual commitment and create positive memories that sustain the relationship.

The importance of touch and physical contact is fundamental in the context of shamanic healing for relationships. Massages with essential oils, such as lavender or rose, can promote intimacy and relaxation, helping to relieve tension and strengthen emotional connection. Massage not only relaxes the body, but also opens up a space for non-verbal communication and the expression of affection and attention.

Creating a space for open dialog is essential for resolving conflicts and promoting mutual understanding. The shaman can guide the partners in the practice of dialog circles, where each person has the opportunity to speak and be heard without interruption. This format promotes active listening and respect, allowing both to express their needs and feelings in a safe and constructive way. The facilitation of these circles can include the use of a talking stick or other symbolic object that marks each person's moment to speak.

Integrating gratitude and celebration practices is fundamental to maintaining positive energy in the relationship. Celebrating small achievements and moments of joy, and expressing gratitude regularly, helps to create an atmosphere of support and appreciation. Practicing gratitude rituals can include creating a "gratitude jar", where each partner writes messages of thanks and places them in the jar to be read at special moments.

Practicing conscious breathing and grounding techniques can help reduce tension and stress in the relationship. Synchronized breathing, where both partners breathe together in a harmonized rhythm, can create a sense of connection and calm. Grounding techniques, such as walking barefoot in nature or meditating outdoors, help to balance energy and promote emotional stability.

The shamanic journey to resolve relationship problems is an ongoing process that involves the integration of various spiritual and holistic practices. By promoting self-knowledge, healing family lineage, strengthening emotional connection, using touch and physical contact, creating spaces for open dialogue, and practicing gratitude and grounding, it is possible to profoundly transform relationship dynamics. These practices not only alleviate existing conflicts, but also create a solid foundation of love, respect and cooperation where both partners can grow and thrive together.

The practice of a reconciliation ritual is fundamental to restoring harmony after significant conflicts. This ritual can take place in a sacred space, prepared with natural elements such as crystals, plants and candles. The shaman guides the partners through a ceremony that involves the honest expression of feelings, the asking and offering of forgiveness, and the reaffirmation of mutual commitments. During the ritual, a shared cup of water or herbal tea can be used as a symbol of purification and renewal.

The creation of a spiritual contract is a shamanic practice that can strengthen the commitment between the partners. This contract can be written together, specifying intentions, commitments and desires for the relationship. Elements such as mutual respect, open communication and emotional support are often included. Signing this contract in a sacred environment and keeping a copy in a visible place helps to remind and reinforce these commitments on a daily basis.

The importance of shadow work in the context of relationship problems cannot be underestimated. The shaman can help partners explore hidden aspects of themselves, known as the "shadow", which may be negatively influencing the relationship. This work involves accepting and integrating these shadow parts, promoting healing and transformation. Practices such as guided meditation and reflective writing can help bring out and process these aspects.

The use of symbols and amulets is a common practice in shamanism for protection and strengthening the relationship. Creating a protective amulet together can serve as a tangible symbol of your union and intention to protect and nurture the relationship. These amulets can be made from natural materials such as stones, crystals, feathers and wood, and can be carried or placed in a meaningful place in the living environment.

Lunar connection rituals are powerful practices that can be performed in tune with the phases of the moon to strengthen the relationship. During the new moon, partners can plant seeds of intention for the relationship, focusing on what they want to cultivate together. On the full moon, they can perform release rituals, leaving behind any negative energy or obstacles that are preventing the relationship from growing. These rituals help to align the relationship with natural cycles and promote harmony and continuous growth.

The practice of sacred dances and movements is another shamanic technique that can help release tension and strengthen emotional connection. Dancing together in a safe and sacred environment, moving to the rhythm of drums or soft music, allows partners to express their emotions non-verbally and creatively. This practice promotes the release of emotional and energetic blockages, creating a harmonious flow of energy between partners.

Participation in community healing circles can provide valuable additional support for individuals and their relationships.

These circles offer a safe space to share experiences, receive guidance and support, and learn new healing practices. The sense of community and belonging can strengthen individuals emotionally, reflecting positively on their personal relationships.

Practicing positive future visualizations can help partners focus on the possibilities and growth of the relationship. Together, they can visualize scenes of a harmonious and happy future, involving shared achievements and moments of joy. These visualizations can be incorporated into regular meditations, reinforcing the intention to create a positive future and strengthening mutual commitment.

Finally, integrating mindfulness practices into the daily routine can help maintain calm and presence in the relationship. Simple techniques such as mindful breathing, short meditations and practicing gratitude can be incorporated into daily activities, promoting an atmosphere of peace and harmony. Mindfulness helps partners to be more present and connected, reducing reactivity and promoting mutual understanding and respect.

The shamanic journey to resolve relationship problems is a holistic and continuous process that involves the integration of various spiritual practices and healing techniques. By practicing reconciliation rituals, spiritual contracts, shadow work, the use of amulets, lunar connection, sacred dances, participation in community circles, positive future visualizations and mindfulness, it is possible to profoundly transform relationship dynamics. These practices not only alleviate existing conflicts, but also create a solid foundation of love, respect and cooperation where both partners can grow and thrive together.

Chapter 15
Sadness and Grief

Sadness and grief are natural emotions that are part of the human experience, especially after the loss of a loved one, a significant change or a traumatic event. These feelings can be deep and long-lasting, affecting every aspect of a person's life. The grieving process is unique to each individual, varying in intensity and duration, but is essential for healing and integrating the loss.

Identifying the symptoms of sadness and grief is crucial to understanding the depth of the emotional impact. Common symptoms include frequent crying, feelings of emptiness, loss of interest in previously pleasurable activities, difficulty sleeping, changes in appetite and feelings of hopelessness. These symptoms can range from mild to severe and, in some cases, can develop into more serious conditions such as depression if not addressed properly.

The impact of grief and bereavement on daily life can be significant, interfering with a person's ability to function normally at work, at school or in other daily activities. It is common to experience a loss of motivation and energy, making it difficult to carry out simple tasks. In addition, grief can affect relationships, creating a sense of isolation and incomprehension on the part of friends and family who may not know how to offer adequate support.

Common causes of grief and bereavement include personal losses, such as the death of a loved one, the end of a relationship, the loss of a job or drastic life changes, such as moving to a new location. In addition, traumatic experiences, such as accidents or natural disasters, can trigger an intense grieving process. It is important to recognize that grief is not limited to death alone; any significant loss can trigger this emotional process.

Preparing for healing rituals is an essential part of the grieving process. These rituals help to honor the memory of what has been lost, facilitating emotional release and acceptance. The choice of materials needed for the ritual depends on personal and cultural preferences and can include candles, incense, photos, symbolic objects and herbs. Creating a sacred environment, free from distractions and full of elements that bring comfort and peace, is fundamental to the ritual's effectiveness.

The best time and place to perform the ritual are also important. Many people choose to perform these rituals at quiet times, such as early in the morning or late in the afternoon, when it is possible to reflect without interruptions. The ideal location can be an outdoor space, such as a garden or natural area, which offers a direct connection with nature and the healing energy of the environment. Alternatively, an indoor space dedicated to meditation and introspection can be just as effective.

Preparing for healing rituals begins with setting a clear intention. The intention is the foundation of any spiritual practice, directing the energy of the ritual towards a specific goal. In the case of bereavement, the intention can be the release of pain, the acceptance of loss or the search for inner peace. Before starting the ritual, take a moment to reflect on this intention, writing it down on a piece of paper or simply holding it in your mind.

The choice of materials for the ritual should reflect the intention and emotional needs of the participant. Candles can symbolize light and hope, incense can purify the environment and herbs such as sage and rosemary can promote healing and protection. Photos and personal objects that recall the loved one or the loss can be placed on the altar as a way of honoring the memory and establishing an emotional connection.

The sacred space for the ritual should be prepared with care. Physically cleansing the space and energetically purifying it by burning sacred herbs is a common practice. Arranging the materials harmoniously on the altar creates an environment conducive to meditation and introspection. Soft lighting, with candles or natural light, helps to create an atmosphere of tranquillity and reverence.

The ritual begins with a guided meditation. This meditation can include deep, controlled breaths, which help to calm the mind and prepare the body for the spiritual experience. Visualizing a safe and sacred place where the participant can find peace and solace is an effective technique. During meditation, it is important to focus on the set intention, allowing the healing energy to flow through the whole being.

Chants and mantras can be integrated into the ritual to reinforce the intention and raise the energetic vibration. Chanting a simple mantra, such as "Om Shanti" (meaning "Peace"), can help center the mind and open the heart to healing. Repeating the mantra several times creates a meditative rhythm that facilitates spiritual connection and emotional release.

During the ritual, it is common to feel a variety of intense emotions. Allowing yourself to feel and express these emotions is fundamental to the healing process. Crying, speaking aloud or writing down thoughts and feelings can be ways of releasing accumulated pain. These emotional expressions are escape valves that allow grief to take its natural course.

Invoking guide or ancestor spirits is a powerful practice in shamanism. Asking for the presence and support of these spiritual beings can bring comfort and guidance. Feeling the presence of ancestors or spirit guides can strengthen the connection with the spirit world and provide a sense of support and protection. This connection helps the person to feel less alone in their grieving process.

After completing the ritual, it is important to have a period of integration and reflection. Sitting in silence, meditating on the experience and writing down any insights or messages received can help consolidate the healing. This time of reflection allows the emotional and spiritual changes to be assimilated and the participant to prepare to apply these changes in daily life.

Maintaining regular self-care practices and rituals can support the grieving process in the long term. Establishing a routine that includes moments of meditation, gratitude and connection with nature helps to maintain emotional balance and promote ongoing healing. Keeping a grief journal where you record thoughts, feelings and progress can be a valuable tool for monitoring the healing process.

Additional healing techniques can complement mourning rituals and offer ongoing support throughout the healing process. One such technique is the use of guided visualizations, which can help transform emotional pain into peace and acceptance. Visualizations that involve healing light, nature or encounters with spirit guides can be particularly effective.

A common guided visualization involves imagining yourself in a quiet and safe place, such as a serene beach or a peaceful forest. Visualizing a golden or white light coming down from the sky and enveloping you, bringing healing and peace, can help relieve emotional pain. During this visualization, you can invite the presence of spirit guides or deceased loved ones, feeling their love and support. This practice can be done daily or whenever intense feelings of sadness arise.

Art therapy is another powerful tool in the grieving process. Creative expression through painting, drawing, writing or music can help release repressed emotions and explore feelings in a safe and constructive way. Creating a piece of art dedicated to the person or situation you have lost can be an act of homage and a way of processing grief. Art allows emotions to flow freely, facilitating emotional healing.

Movement also plays an important role in healing grief. Physical activities such as dancing, yoga or walks in nature can help release built-up tension and connect with the body in a healthy way. Dancing, in particular, can be a powerful way of expressing emotions that are difficult to verbalize. Dancing to meaningful music or simply moving freely to the rhythm of nature can provide a deep emotional release.

Community connection and social support are crucial during the grieving process. Participating in support groups or healing circles can provide a safe space to share experiences and receive comfort from others who are going through similar situations. These groups offer a sense of belonging and validation, reducing the feeling of isolation often associated with bereavement.

Shamanic healing circles are especially effective, as they combine community support with deep spiritual practices. During these gatherings, it is common to perform group healing rituals, such as chanting, guided meditations and invoking guide spirits. The collective energy of the group can amplify the healing process, offering strength and comfort to the participants.

The practice of gratitude, even in times of mourning, can be a powerful tool for transforming one's emotional outlook. Taking a moment each day to reflect on positive aspects of life and express gratitude can help reorient the mind towards a more positive state. Keeping a gratitude journal, where you write down small blessings and moments of joy, can help balance feelings of sadness and promote a sense of hope.

Connecting with nature is a fundamental practice in shamanism and can be extremely beneficial during bereavement. Spending time outdoors, surrounded by trees, rivers and mountains, can provide a sense of peace and renewal. Nature has an intrinsic healing power, and simply being present in a natural environment can help restore emotional balance. Walking barefoot on the earth, sitting by a river or watching the sunset are simple practices that can bring comfort and clarity.

Integrating healing rituals into the daily routine is essential to support the grieving process. Establishing regular times for meditation, gratitude and spiritual practices helps to create a sense of stability and continuity. These rituals not only offer moments of reflection and healing, but also reinforce the connection with the sacred, providing a firm spiritual foundation during times of change and loss.

Self-care practices are fundamental to supporting the grieving process and promoting emotional and physical well-being. Engaging in activities that nourish the body, mind and spirit helps maintain resilience during difficult times. Adopting healthy habits and creating daily self-care routines can provide a solid foundation for healing.

One essential self-care practice is healthy eating. Consuming a balanced diet, rich in fruits, vegetables, lean proteins and whole grains, provides the body with the nutrients it needs to function optimally. Avoiding processed foods, refined sugars and excessive caffeine can help stabilize energy levels and improve mood. Adequate hydration is also crucial; drinking plenty of water throughout the day supports all bodily functions and contributes to mental clarity.

Sleep is another vital aspect of self-care. Loss can significantly affect sleep patterns, making it difficult to fall asleep or maintain a deep sleep. Establishing a consistent sleep routine, going to bed and waking up at the same time every day, can help regulate the circadian rhythm. Creating an environment conducive to sleep, with a dark, quiet and cool room, and avoiding the use of electronics before bedtime, promotes restful rest.

Regular physical exercise is also beneficial for emotional health. Activities such as walking, running, yoga or tai chi not only strengthen the body, but also help release endorphins, natural chemicals that improve mood. Gentle exercises, such as stretching or mindful movements, can be especially useful for releasing accumulated physical and emotional tension.

Meditation and mindfulness are powerful self-care practices that help calm the mind and reduce stress. Taking a few minutes every day to meditate, focusing on your breathing and observing your thoughts without judgment, can provide a sense of peace and clarity. Practicing mindfulness during everyday activities, such as eating, walking or bathing, helps to keep the focus on the present moment, reducing anxiety and promoting a state of tranquillity.

Social connection is an essential component of self-care during bereavement. Keeping in touch with friends and family who offer emotional support can provide a sense of belonging and security. Taking part in social activities, however simple, such as having coffee with a friend or joining a common interest group, helps to combat isolation and loneliness.

Daily gratitude rituals can be integrated into the self-care routine. Taking a moment every morning or evening to reflect on three things you are grateful for helps refocus the mind on positive aspects of life. Gratitude promotes a mindset of abundance and can help balance feelings of sadness, providing a sense of contentment and peace.

Setting healthy boundaries is crucial for maintaining emotional well-being. Learning to say "no" when necessary and creating space to take care of yourself are important practices. This can include limiting time on social media, avoiding stressful situations or simply setting aside time to relax and recharge.

Practicing hobbies and activities that bring joy is also an effective form of self-care. Dedicating time to pleasurable activities such as reading, cooking, gardening, painting or playing a musical instrument can provide a healthy distraction and a way to express emotions. These activities help to connect with what brings happiness and personal satisfaction.

Continuously integrating the lessons learned during the grieving process is crucial to maintaining long-term well-being. Spiritual and self-care practices should be seen as integral parts of daily life, not just temporary measures. Maintaining these practices helps to sustain healing and promote an ongoing sense of balance and peace.

Creating a permanent sacred space in the home can be an effective way of integrating these practices into the daily routine. This space can be a small altar with elements that symbolize healing and spiritual connection, such as crystals, candles, incense and meaningful personal objects. Taking a few minutes every day to meditate or perform small rituals in this space helps maintain the connection with the sacred and reinforce the intention to heal.

The regular practice of meditation remains a powerful tool for maintaining inner peace. Meditating daily, even for a few minutes, helps to calm the mind, reduce stress and promote mental clarity. Meditation can be complemented with guided visualizations of healing light or meetings with spirit guides, providing a continuous sense of support and protection.

Gratitude should be an ongoing practice. Keeping a gratitude journal, where you regularly record the things you are grateful for, helps you cultivate a positive mindset and focus on the positive aspects of life. This simple practice can have a profound impact on emotional well-being, helping to balance feelings of sadness and promoting a sense of contentment.

Connecting with nature should be maintained as an integral part of the self-care routine. Spending time outdoors, in contact with the earth, water and fresh air, provides energy renewal and a sense of peace. Activities such as gardening, walking in parks or simply sitting outside help to maintain a connection with the natural world and absorb nature's healing energy.

Rituals of release and renewal are important for sustaining healing in the long term. Performing periodic rituals, such as during the full and new moon phases, helps to release accumulated negative energies and set new intentions for the future. These rituals can include burning sacred herbs, creating sand mandalas or performing water purification ceremonies.

Ongoing participation in healing circles or support groups can provide valuable emotional support. These gatherings offer the opportunity to share experiences, receive support and guidance and strengthen a sense of belonging. The collective energy of a group can amplify the healing process and provide a sense of community.

Practicing personal rituals, such as lighting a candle in honor of a loved one or writing letters that will never be sent, can help process feelings of loss in a constructive way. These rituals allow the person to express their emotions and find ways to honor the memory of what has been lost.

Developing a personalized self-care plan is an effective strategy for maintaining well-being. This plan can include activities and practices that nourish the body, mind and spirit, adapted to individual needs and preferences. Reviewing and adjusting this plan regularly helps to ensure that it remains relevant and effective over time.

Seeking new forms of personal and spiritual growth is also an important part of continuous integration. Attending workshops, reading books on spirituality and healing, and exploring new spiritual practices can offer new perspectives and tools for growth. Continuous learning and spiritual exploration help to deepen the connection with the sacred and promote ongoing personal development.

Finally, it is essential to practice self-compassion and acceptance throughout the grieving process. Recognizing that healing is an ongoing process and that it is normal to have ups and downs helps to maintain a healthy perspective. Treating yourself with kindness and understanding, celebrating small progress and being patient with yourself, is fundamental to sustaining healing in the long term.

Chapter 16
Lack of Purpose

Lack of purpose is a feeling of disconnection and disorientation that can profoundly affect a person's life. Feeling directionless or without a clear goal can lead to a lack of motivation, discontent and even depression. In shamanism, life purpose is seen as a unique and personal spiritual journey, where each individual must discover and follow their path in an authentic and meaningful way.

To identify a lack of purpose, it's important to recognize the common symptoms associated with this condition. Individuals who feel a lack of purpose often report a sense of inner emptiness, apathy and a loss of interest in activities that were once meaningful. This disconnection can manifest as procrastination, lack of motivation, feelings of worthlessness and an absence of clear goals in life. In addition, a lack of purpose can negatively impact mental and emotional health, increasing vulnerability to stress, anxiety and depression.

The cause of purposelessness is multifaceted and can vary from person to person. It is often related to a spiritual disconnection, where the individual has lost touch with their beliefs, values and the essence of their identity. This can occur due to past traumas, significant life changes, or simply not dedicating enough time to exploring and understanding their own spiritual path. A lack of direction in life can also be exacerbated by external pressures, such as social and family expectations, which can distract a person from their true purpose.

Preparation for the shamanic healing ritual begins with creating an environment conducive to introspection and spiritual reconnection. This space should be quiet and free of distractions, allowing for a deep connection with the spiritual world. Elements such as crystals, incense, candles and sacred symbols can be used to create an altar that symbolizes the intention to rediscover one's purpose in life.

The practice of meditation is a powerful tool for finding clarity and direction. Guided meditations that involve visualizations of a path or a journey can be particularly useful. Visualizing yourself walking along an enlightened path, where each step leads to a greater understanding of yourself and your life purpose, can bring valuable insights. During these meditations, it is important to keep an open and receptive mind, allowing answers to come intuitively.

In addition, the use of chants and mantras can help raise the vibration of the ritual and promote a deeper connection with the inner self. Traditional shamanic chants or mantras that resonate with the intention of discovery and clarity can be repeated during meditation and ritual. These sacred sounds help to calm the mind, open the heart and align the spirit with the greater purpose.

Another important aspect is the practice of intuitive writing or journaling. Writing about personal thoughts, feelings and reflections can be an effective way of exploring and clarifying one's life purpose. Questions such as "What am I really passionate about?" "What are my unique talents?" and "How can I serve the world in a meaningful way?" can guide the writing and bring out deep and authentic answers.

Integrating these practices into daily life helps sustain the process of rediscovering one's life purpose. Attending spiritual workshops, reading inspiring books and seeking the guidance of experienced mentors or shamans can offer additional support. These activities not only enrich personal understanding, but also provide practical tools and techniques for staying aligned with one's life purpose.

The journey to find one's life purpose is continuous and involves the integration of various spiritual practices that promote self-discovery and alignment with one's inner essence. In shamanism, this journey is deeply personal and unique, requiring a sincere and authentic connection with the inner self and spiritual guides.

A fundamental technique for deepening this connection is shamanic journeying. During this practice, the shaman or practitioner enters an altered state of consciousness, usually induced by the rhythmic sound of the drum or rattle. This state allows them to travel to the spirit world, where they can meet guides, power animals and other spiritual beings who offer wisdom and guidance. The shamanic journey can be directed specifically at discovering one's life purpose, asking the guides to reveal insights and paths that bring clarity and direction.

During the journey, it is important to maintain a clear and open intention, allowing the visions and messages to flow naturally. The images and symbols that appear can be powerful and meaningful, offering clues about the way forward. After the journey, it is useful to record all the experiences and insights in a journal, reflecting on the meaning of each element and how it relates to the search for purpose.

Healing and purification rituals also play a crucial role in rediscovering one's life purpose. Smoking with sacred herbs such as sage, cedar or palo santo can help clear stagnant energies and open up the space for new insights. These rituals can be performed regularly to keep the environment and personal aura clean and receptive to spiritual guidance.

Connecting with nature is an essential practice in shamanism and can be a rich source of inspiration and clarity. Spending time in natural environments, such as forests, mountains or near bodies of water, can help restore inner balance and harmony. Nature has an inherent healing power and simply being in a natural environment can promote the peace and introspection needed to discover one's purpose in life.

An effective practice is to take meditative walks in nature, where you walk in silence, observing and absorbing the energy of the surrounding environment. During these walks, it is useful to maintain the intention of finding clarity and guidance, allowing the mind to calm down and the connection with the spirit to strengthen. Answers can come through sensations, thoughts or even signs in nature, such as the appearance of a specific animal or a pattern of light.

The use of sacred symbols and artifacts can also help to keep the focus on the search for purpose. Creating a personal altar with objects that symbolize the spiritual journey, such as crystals, feathers, shells and images of power animals, can serve as an anchor point for daily practice. These objects are not just decorative; they carry deep meanings and energies that can support the intention of self-discovery and spiritual alignment.

Crystals, in particular, are powerful tools for healing and clarification. Crystals such as amethyst, which promotes intuition and peace, and sodalite, which helps with communication and inner truth, can be used during meditation and rituals. Holding these crystals or placing them on the body can amplify the healing energy and help open the third eye and the heart, centers of intuition and love.

The practice of creative visualization is another valuable technique for discovering and manifesting one's life purpose. During meditation, you can visualize your ideal life, seeing yourself living according to your purpose and feeling the emotions associated with this realization. Visualizing every detail, from daily activities to interactions with other people, can help clarify what you really want and how you can achieve this state of being.

In addition to these practices, it is essential to seek the support and guidance of experienced spiritual mentors or shamans. Participating in healing circles, workshops and retreats can provide a supportive and learning environment where you can share experiences and receive valuable insights. Exchanging wisdom and connecting with other spiritual seekers enriches the journey and strengthens the determination to follow the path of one's life purpose.

Integrating these practices into daily life helps sustain the process of discovery and alignment with one's life purpose. By cultivating a regular spiritual routine, which includes meditation, rituals, connecting with nature and seeking community support, it is possible to stay connected with the inner self and spiritual guides, allowing the journey to unfold in an authentic and meaningful way.

In addition to the spiritual practices mentioned above, it is essential to incorporate a holistic and integrative approach to finding and maintaining one's life purpose. This includes taking care of the body, mind and spirit in a balanced way, recognizing the interconnectedness between all aspects of being.

Conscious eating plays a vital role in maintaining energetic and spiritual balance. Opting for a diet rich in natural foods, such as fruit, vegetables, whole grains and lean proteins, can help keep the body healthy and the mind clear. Avoiding processed foods and those rich in refined sugars can reduce inflammation in the body and promote a more stable mental state. In addition, the practice of blessing food before meals can increase spiritual connection, expressing gratitude for the nourishment received and the vital energy present in food.

Regular physical exercise is also essential to keep body and mind in harmony. Activities such as yoga, tai chi and walking not only strengthen the body, but also promote mental calm and spiritual clarity. These practices help to release accumulated tension, increase flexibility and improve the circulation of vital energy. Integrating mindful movement into the daily routine can create a space for introspection and connection with inner purpose.

Adequate sleep is another crucial component in maintaining spiritual and emotional balance. Ensuring quality rest helps regenerate the body and mind, preparing them for the daily journey in search of life's purpose. Establishing a consistent nighttime routine, including relaxation practices such as meditation, reading inspiring books and applying calming essential oils, can promote deep, restorative sleep.

Practicing daily gratitude is a powerful tool for maintaining a positive attitude and focusing on life's purpose. Taking a moment at the end of the day to reflect on the things you are grateful for can transform your perspective and increase your emotional resilience. Keeping a gratitude journal, where you write down three things you are grateful for every day, can create a mental state of contentment and peace, facilitating clarity and motivation to follow the path of purpose.

Creative expression is another valuable practice for discovering one's life purpose. Activities such as writing, painting, music and dance allow the expression of deep emotions and thoughts, helping to clarify what really matters. Artistic creation can be a form of active meditation, exploring the subconscious and revealing insights into one's spiritual path. Allowing yourself to experience different forms of art without judgment can open new doors to self-understanding and personal fulfillment.

The search for knowledge and continuous learning is also fundamental on the journey to finding one's life purpose. Reading books, attending lectures, participating in workshops and courses on spirituality, self-knowledge and personal development can offer new perspectives and tools for the journey. Continuous learning keeps the mind open and curious, promoting personal and spiritual growth.

Practicing mindfulness is an effective technique for staying focused on the present and reducing mental distraction. Mindfulness involves being fully present in the moment, observing thoughts and sensations without judgment. This can be practiced through short meditations throughout the day or simply by taking a few minutes to breathe deeply and reconnect with the present. The regular practice of mindfulness helps to reduce emotional reactivity and create a space of inner calm, facilitating clarity and direction in life.

Creating a spiritual support network is also essential for maintaining one's life purpose. Connecting with other people who share spiritual interests and values can offer support, inspiration and motivation. Participating in meditation groups, healing circles or spiritual communities provides a sense of belonging and emotional support, strengthening the individual journey.

The role of rituals and ceremonies in daily life cannot be underestimated. Performing regular rituals, such as full and new moon ceremonies, celebrations of seasonal changes and gratitude rituals, can create a rhythm and structure that supports the spiritual journey. These rituals help to mark time and celebrate the changes and cycles of life, offering moments of reflection and renewal.

The journey to discovering and maintaining one's life purpose is not linear and can be full of challenges and moments of deep introspection. It is essential to approach this journey with an open mind and a receptive heart, allowing yourself to explore different paths and practices that resonate with your inner self.

One of the most enriching practices is participating in shamanic ceremonies. These ceremonies, which can include full moon rituals, drum journeys, healing circles and purification ceremonies, offer opportunities to deepen the spiritual connection and receive guidance from the guiding spirits. Each ceremony is a unique experience that can bring new insights into life purpose and help realign the person with their spiritual path.

During these ceremonies, the use of entheogenic plants, such as ayahuasca or peyote, can be incorporated under the guidance of an experienced shaman. These plants are known for their healing properties and for promoting altered states of consciousness that facilitate introspection and spiritual connection. It is important to approach the use of these plants with respect and proper preparation, recognizing their power and potential to reveal deep truths about life purpose.

In addition to ceremonies, practicing daily personal rituals can help maintain the connection with life purpose. These rituals can be simple and include activities such as lighting a candle and setting an intention for the day, meditating at sunrise, or offering gratitude to nature. Maintaining these rituals can create a sense of continuity and purpose, reinforcing spiritual connection and clarity about the path ahead.

Practicing oracles, such as tarot or rune reading, can also offer valuable insights into life purpose. These methods of divination have been used for centuries to gain spiritual guidance and clarity on personal issues. When consulting an oracle, it is essential to set a clear intention and be open to the messages received, interpreting them with wisdom and discernment.

Exploring personal talents and passions is a fundamental part of discovering one's life purpose. Identifying activities that bring joy and satisfaction can be an indicator of direction. Whether through art, music, teaching, caring for others, or any other activity that resonates with the heart, following these passions can lead to a path more aligned with life purpose. Regular practice of these activities not only brings personal fulfillment, but can also reveal new opportunities and paths to explore.

Developing the skills of self-compassion and self-acceptance is crucial during this journey. Often, a lack of purpose can be accompanied by feelings of inadequacy or self-doubt. Practices such as compassionate meditation, where you send love and kindness to yourself and others, can help transform these feelings. Cultivating a kind and encouraging inner voice promotes emotional healing and strengthens the determination to follow the path of life purpose.

The support of mentors and spiritual guides is another valuable tool. Seeking guidance from people with more experience in the spiritual journey can provide insights, encouragement and practical support. These mentors can offer fresh perspectives and help overcome obstacles, sharing wisdom and experiences that light the way.

Participating in spiritual retreats offers an opportunity for deep immersion and a break from the distractions of everyday life. These retreats, which can last from a few days to several weeks, allow for intense concentration on spiritual practices and self-discovery. The retreat environment, often located in places of natural beauty and tranquillity, offers the ideal space for reflection and deep connection with one's life purpose.

The practice of guided visualizations can continue to be a powerful tool for clarifying life purpose. Visualizations that involve encounters with the future self, where you see yourself fully living your purpose, can help solidify the vision and create an action plan to achieve this state. These visualizations can be done on a daily basis, continually reinforcing the intention to live in line with one's life purpose.

Integrating these practices and attitudes into daily life promotes a continuous state of discovery and alignment with life purpose. The journey to find and live according to purpose is one of the most profound and rewarding one can undertake, providing not only personal satisfaction, but also a significant contribution to the world around us.

The journey to finding and living one's life purpose is an ongoing exploration that requires dedication, openness and integrative practices. In the final phase of this chapter, we will cover additional strategies that complement the previous practices, further strengthening the connection with life purpose.

One important practice is the creation of a "Life Vision". This involves writing down in detail what you want your life to be like, including aspects such as career, relationships, health, spiritual growth and contributions to the community. The Life Vision serves as a map that guides daily decisions and actions, keeping the focus on what is truly meaningful. Revisiting and updating this vision periodically allows one to adjust course as necessary, reflecting new insights and personal evolutions.

In addition, the practice of "Inspired Actions" is fundamental to turning the vision into reality. This means taking concrete steps in line with your life purpose. These actions can be small, such as reading a book related to your interests or taking part in a workshop, or larger, such as changing careers or starting a passion project. The key is that these actions are in harmony with your life vision and bring a sense of progress and accomplishment.

The concept of "Natural Rhythm" is another crucial aspect. Respecting and working with the natural rhythms of the body and nature can provide a solid foundation for discovering one's life purpose. This includes practices such as observing and honoring the lunar cycles, the seasons and one's own circadian rhythms. Integrating these observations into daily life can bring a sense of alignment and fluidity, making it easier to connect with purpose.

The practice of "Authentic Communication" is vital for living according to one's life purpose. This involves expressing thoughts, feelings and needs in an honest and respectful way, both with yourself and with others. Authentic communication strengthens relationships and creates an environment of mutual support, which is essential for maintaining purpose. Learning to say "no" to activities and relationships that don't resonate with purpose and "yes" to those that nurture it is a powerful skill.

"Celebration rituals" are equally important. Celebrating achievements and milestones on the path to life purpose, no matter how small, reinforces progress and maintains motivation. These celebrations can be private, as a moment of gratitude or reflection, or shared with friends and family. Acknowledging and honoring each step taken strengthens determination and joy in the journey.

"Constant reflection" is a practice that involves regularly setting aside time to review and reflect on progress. This can be done through journaling, meditation or conversations with a mentor or trusted friend. Reflection allows you to adjust your trajectory as necessary, ensuring that your actions and decisions remain aligned with your life purpose. It's a time to identify what's working, what needs to change and how you can continue to grow and evolve.

The integration of "Service to Others" is also a significant part of living with purpose. Getting involved in activities that benefit other people and the community can bring a deep sense of meaning and connection. This can include volunteer work, mentoring, or simply everyday acts of kindness. Serving others not only enriches the lives of those who receive, but also strengthens one's own connection to purpose, bringing a sense of interconnectedness and contribution.

Finally, "Flexibility and Resilience" are essential qualities for the journey of discovering and maintaining one's life purpose. Being open to change and adaptation, accepting that the path may not be linear and learning to pick yourself up after setbacks are crucial skills. Resilience allows you to face challenges with grace and determination, while flexibility makes it easier to adapt to new circumstances and opportunities that arise along the way.

The journey to finding and living one's life purpose is rich and multifaceted, requiring an ongoing commitment to personal and spiritual growth. By integrating these practices into daily life, it is possible to create a solid foundation for self-discovery and fulfillment. Maintaining your life purpose provides not only personal satisfaction, but also the opportunity to make a significant difference in the world around you.

Chapter 17
Financial Problems

Financial problems are a common source of stress and anxiety, profoundly impacting a person's mental and emotional health. Identifying and addressing the underlying causes of these problems is essential to promoting well-being and financial stability.

Identifying the symptoms of financial problems can help to understand the extent of the impact they have on a person's life. Common symptoms include constant worry about money, difficulties paying bills, mounting debt and the feeling of being trapped in a cycle of scarcity. These problems can lead to a range of emotional complications, such as anxiety, depression and conflicts in relationships.

The impact on mental health is significant, as worrying about finances can result in sleepless nights, loss of appetite and difficulties concentrating. The constant pressure to balance finances can affect performance at work and the ability to make informed decisions. It is important to recognize that financial problems not only affect the individual, but also their family and social relationships.

Common causes of financial problems include a lack of proper planning, uncontrolled spending and unforeseen financial events. The lack of a clear and realistic budget can lead to debt and the inability to save for emergencies. In addition, impulsive or unnecessary spending can aggravate the situation, making it difficult to achieve financial stability.

Preparation for the healing ritual begins with creating a peaceful environment conducive to introspection. This space should be organized to promote calm and concentration, using elements that symbolize abundance and prosperity. Meditation and reflection on attitudes towards money are important initial steps towards understanding and transforming negative financial patterns.

During the ritual, you can use crystals, candles and incense that represent prosperity and financial stability. Creating an altar with these elements can help focus the intention of healing and transformation. The use of mantras and chants that reinforce financial security can be incorporated into the ritual, helping to raise energy and promote a positive mental state.

In addition, visualizing a stable and prosperous financial future can be a powerful tool. Imagining yourself living debt-free, with adequate savings and the ability to deal with financial emergencies can help reprogram the mind to adopt healthier financial habits. During this visualization, it is important to feel the emotions associated with security and financial freedom, reinforcing these sensations in the subconscious.

The healing ritual for financial problems should be seen as a step in a continuous process of transformation and growth. Adopting daily practices that promote financial responsibility, such as keeping a budget, avoiding unnecessary spending and seeking knowledge about personal finances, is crucial to sustaining the desired changes.

To deepen the healing of financial problems, it is essential to integrate spiritual practices with practical financial management strategies. Combining these approaches can provide a more holistic and sustainable path to achieving financial stability and prosperity.

A fundamental practice is the creation of a detailed and realistic budget. The budget is an essential tool for understanding the current financial situation and planning for the future. It helps to identify all sources of income and list all expenses, from basic needs to discretionary spending. Keeping an up-to-date budget allows you to track spending and adjust as necessary to avoid getting into debt.

In addition to creating a budget, it is important to set clear and achievable financial goals. Goals should be specific, measurable, attainable, relevant and time-bound (SMART). This could include creating an emergency fund, reducing debt, saving for a significant purchase or investing in education or personal development. Having well-defined financial goals helps keep you focused and motivated to stick to the plan.

The regular practice of meditation and visualization can also help reinforce a mindset of abundance and prosperity. During meditation, visualize yourself achieving your financial goals and living in a state of security and comfort. Feel the joy and tranquillity that come with financial freedom. This exercise not only calms the mind, but also reprograms the subconscious to adopt attitudes and behaviors that promote financial health.

Gratitude rituals are another powerful practice. Gratitude has the power to transform the perception of scarcity into a sense of abundance. Taking a few minutes every day to reflect on and give thanks for financial blessings, no matter how small, can help change your perspective and attract more prosperity. Keeping a financial gratitude journal can be an effective daily practice.

In the shamanic context, connecting with nature can provide valuable insights into abundance and sustainability. Spending time outdoors, meditating in a natural environment and making offerings of gratitude to the earth can help strengthen the spiritual connection to prosperity. Nature is a constant reminder that abundance is available to all who align with its energies and rhythms.

The use of specific crystals and plants can also support financial healing. Crystals such as citrine, pyrite and jade are known for their properties of attracting abundance and prosperity. These crystals can be placed on the altar, carried in the pocket or worn as jewelry to keep the intention of prosperity ever present. Plants such as basil, mint and rosemary are also associated with abundance and can be grown at home or used in purification rituals.

Working with positive affirmations is an effective technique for transforming limiting beliefs about money. Affirmations such as "I am worthy of abundance", "Prosperity flows to me easily" and "I manage my finances wisely" can be repeated daily to reinforce a positive mindset towards money. These affirmations can be said out loud, written in a diary or displayed in visible places for constant reminder.

Financial education is another important pillar for curing financial problems. Investing time in learning about personal finance, debt management, investments and economics can empower people to make informed decisions and build a solid financial foundation. Attending workshops, reading books and consulting financial experts are effective ways of acquiring knowledge and practical skills.

Integrating these spiritual and strategic practices can create a solid path to financial healing. In the next segment, we'll explore how to deal with emotional and psychological obstacles that can arise during the financial healing journey, as well as delve into specific shamanic techniques for transforming your relationship with money and prosperity.

Dealing with emotional and psychological obstacles is crucial for financial healing, as the roots of financial problems are often deeply linked to personal emotions and beliefs. Transforming your relationship with money begins with identifying and overcoming these internal barriers.

One of the first steps is an honest self-assessment of limiting beliefs about money. Beliefs such as "money is the root of all evil", "I'll never have enough" or "I'm not good at handling money" can create significant blockages. Recognizing these beliefs is the first step towards transforming them. The shaman can help with this transformation through rituals and journeys that reveal and release these limiting beliefs.

The practice of self-compassion is essential during this process. Many people blame themselves for their financial difficulties, which can lead to feelings of shame and inadequacy. It's important to treat yourself with kindness and recognize that everyone faces financial challenges at some point. Self-compassion involves forgiving yourself for past mistakes and focusing on learning and growing.

Creating a safe space to explore and release negative emotions associated with money is a vital part of financial healing. This can be done through techniques such as therapeutic writing, where you freely express all your feelings about money and finances. Burning or burying these writings can symbolize the release of these emotions, creating space for new perspectives and opportunities.

Participating in financial support groups or healing circles can provide a sense of community and support. Sharing experiences and strategies with others facing similar challenges can be encouraging and inspiring. These groups offer a safe space to openly discuss financial issues without judgment and to receive emotional support.

Developing a practical action plan is essential for overcoming financial problems. This plan should include concrete and achievable steps, such as reducing expenses, increasing income or negotiating debts. Breaking the plan down into smaller goals and celebrating each achievement along the way can help maintain motivation and progress.

In addition to the practical aspects, incorporating energy healing techniques can be highly beneficial. Practices such as Reiki therapy, pranic healing or acupuncture can help release energetic blockages that impact financial health. The shaman can work with the individual's energy field to restore balance and harmony, promoting a sense of well-being and the ability to attract prosperity.

Financial protection visualization is a powerful technique for creating an energy shield around yourself. Visualizing a protective light enveloping your body and environment can help ward off negative influences and create a safe space for prosperity. Repeating this visualization daily can strengthen the intention of protection and financial security.

Strengthening the relationship with money can be promoted through gratitude rituals and offerings. Giving thanks for the money you already have, regardless of the amount, can change your perspective from one of scarcity to one of abundance. Making small offerings, such as donations to charities or helping someone in need, can create a positive flow of energy, reinforcing the belief in abundance.

Financial purification rituals, such as cleaning up the physical and digital environment, are also important. Organizing financial documents, paying overdue bills and eliminating unnecessary expenses are all ways to cleanse stagnant energy. Digital cleaning, including organizing files and deleting unwanted emails, can create a sense of order and control.

Practicing financial mindfulness is another effective tool. Being present and aware during financial transactions, avoiding impulsive purchases and making deliberate decisions can significantly improve money management. Mindfulness helps create a space between impulse and action, allowing for more conscious choices in line with financial goals.

By integrating these emotional, energetic and practical practices, you can transform your relationship with money and create a solid foundation for financial prosperity. In the next segment, we'll explore the importance of continuous financial education and how to maintain motivation and progress over time, as well as specific shamanic techniques for attracting and maintaining abundance.

Ongoing financial education is a crucial element in the journey of healing financial problems. Learning about personal finance and acquiring new skills can empower and transform your relationship with money. It is important to adopt a continuous learning approach, constantly seeking new information and strategies to improve financial management.

There are various resources available for financial education, including books, online courses, seminars and workshops. Participating in these programs can provide practical knowledge about budgeting, saving, investing and debt management. Books such as "Rich Dad, Poor Dad" by Robert Kiyosaki and "The Richest Man in Babylon" by George S. Clason are classics that offer valuable lessons on how to build wealth and manage money effectively.

Another important practice is to keep up with economic and financial trends. Keeping up to date with economic news and financial market developments can help you make informed decisions about investments and financial strategies. Subscribing to financial newsletters and following financial experts on social media are effective ways to stay informed.

Motivation and progress on the financial healing journey can be maintained through regular practices of reviewing and adjusting financial plans. Reviewing the budget monthly, evaluating progress against financial goals and making adjustments as necessary are essential steps. Celebrating small victories, such as paying off a debt or reaching a savings goal, can reinforce motivation and confidence.

Creating a solid support system is also vital. Having someone to be accountable to, be it a partner, friend or financial mentor, can provide emotional and motivational support. Sharing financial goals and discussing challenges and successes with someone you trust can help maintain focus and discipline.

In the shamanic context, specific rituals can be performed to attract and maintain abundance. One example is the new moon ritual, which is a powerful time to plant new intentions and start afresh. During the new moon, the shaman can guide the creation of a ritual in which financial intentions are written on a piece of paper, visualizing them as already fulfilled. This paper can be placed on an altar or buried in the ground as a symbol of growth and fertility.

Another powerful ritual is to create a mandala of abundance. Mandalas are symbolic designs that represent the universe and can be used as tools for meditation and manifestation. Creating an abundance mandala with elements that symbolize prosperity, such as coins, precious stones and symbols of wealth, can help focus the mind and energy on attracting abundance. Meditating regularly with the mandala can reinforce this intention and manifest positive results.

The practice of offerings and donations also plays a significant role in maintaining the flow of abundance. Donating a portion of earnings to causes that matter can create a cycle of positive energy and reinforce the belief in abundance. Regularly practicing generosity, whether through financial donations or donations of time and skills, can open doors to new opportunities and increase the feeling of prosperity.

Connecting with nature and the elements can also be used to attract prosperity. Performing rituals outdoors, such as meditations by rivers, forests or mountains, can strengthen the connection with the earth and its abundant energies. Using natural elements such as running water or precious stones in rituals can amplify the intention to attract prosperity and financial stability.

The practice of financial mindfulness, as mentioned above, helps to maintain full attention during all financial transactions. Making conscious and deliberate decisions about spending and investments prevents impulsivity and promotes financial discipline. Setting aside specific times of the day to review finances and plan spending can create a routine of responsibility and control.

Overcoming unexpected financial challenges and crises requires a combined approach of shamanic practices and practical strategies. These moments can be stressful and challenging, but with the right tools, it is possible to maintain resilience and financial stability.

The first step is to create an emergency fund. This fund should be set aside to cover unexpected expenses, such as home repairs, medical bills or loss of income. Ideally, an emergency fund should cover at least three to six months of basic expenses. Building up this fund can be done gradually, earmarking a portion of monthly income for savings until the goal is reached.

The practice of financial mindfulness remains crucial during crises. Remaining calm and focused helps you make rational decisions and avoid panic. Daily meditation and deep breathing exercises can help reduce stress and maintain mental clarity.

In the shamanic context, specific rituals can be performed to obtain guidance and spiritual support during financial crises. The shamanic journey is a powerful tool for gaining insights and solutions. During the journey, the shaman can seek advice from spirit guides on how to deal with the financial situation. These guides can offer wisdom and support to help navigate difficult times.

Another effective ritual is one of financial purification and protection. Performing a ritual to cleanse the financial environment energetically can help remove blockages and open up paths to new opportunities. This can include burning sacred herbs such as sage or cedar to purify the space, followed by a visualization of protective light around the financial environment. This ritual can be done regularly to keep the space clean and protected.

The practice of positive affirmations is especially important during financial crises. Repeating affirmations such as "I am resilient and capable of overcoming any financial challenge" or "Prosperity is on the way, even in difficult times" can help maintain a positive and empowered mindset. These affirmations can be repeated several times a day, written in a diary or displayed in visible places to reinforce confidence and faith in one's ability to overcome.

The support network also plays a vital role during financial crises. Seeking support from friends, family or community groups can offer emotional comfort and sometimes practical assistance. Sharing concerns and seeking advice from trusted people can help ease the emotional burden and provide new perspectives and solutions.

Continuing education about finances is key to dealing with crises. Seeking information on how to manage debts, negotiate with creditors and find financial resources can be extremely helpful. There are many organizations and financial advisors that offer free or low-cost guidance to help in times of need.

Connecting with nature can be a source of strength and inspiration during financial crises. Spending time outdoors, meditating in natural surroundings and performing rituals of gratitude to the earth can help restore inner peace and mental clarity. Nature offers a space of tranquillity and renewal that can be extremely beneficial in times of stress.

Gratitude rituals are especially important during financial crises. Regularly practicing gratitude helps you focus on existing abundance and attract more positive aspects. Taking a few minutes every day to reflect on financial blessings, no matter how small, can change perspective and increase emotional resilience.

Flexibility and adaptation are essential for overcoming financial crises. Being willing to adjust plans and strategies as necessary is crucial. This can include reducing expenses, looking for additional sources of income or renegotiating debts. Maintaining a proactive and adaptable approach helps to face challenges more effectively.

Finally, self-care is vital during financial crises. Taking care of physical, mental and emotional health helps maintain energy and resilience. Practicing activities that promote well-being, such as physical exercise, relaxing hobbies and leisure time with loved ones, can provide the balance needed to face financial challenges with strength and clarity.

By integrating these shamanic practices and practical strategies, it is possible to overcome unexpected financial challenges and crises while maintaining resilience and financial stability. The journey of financial healing is continuous and requires dedication, constant learning and a holistic approach that addresses all aspects of being. With these tools, you can transform your relationship with money and create a life of prosperity and balance.

Chapter 18
Addictions and Dependencies

Addictions and dependencies are complex issues that affect a person's physical, mental and spiritual health. They can involve substances such as alcohol, drugs and medication, or behaviors such as gambling, the internet and compulsive shopping. Recognizing an addiction is the first crucial step towards healing.

Addictions often arise as a way of escaping emotional pain, trauma or stress. They offer a temporary escape, but in the long term, they can lead to devastating consequences. Identifying the signs of addiction is essential to starting on a path to recovery. Common signs include increased tolerance to the substance or behavior, withdrawal symptoms, loss of control over use or behavior, and continued use despite negative consequences.

In the shamanic context, healing from addictions involves a holistic approach that considers the individual as a whole - body, mind and spirit. This means addressing not only the physical symptoms of addiction, but also the underlying emotional and spiritual causes. The journey to recovery is seen as a process of reconnecting with one's essence and with the spiritual world.

Preparation for the healing process begins with the creation of a safe and sacred space. This space should be peaceful and free of distractions, allowing for a deep connection with one's spiritual guides and essence. Elements such as crystals, herbs and spiritual symbols can be used to raise the energy of the environment. Purifying the space by burning sacred herbs, such as sage or palo santo, can help clear negative energies and create an atmosphere of peace and introspection.

In addition, it is important to recognize and understand the underlying causes of addictions and dependencies. They are often linked to unresolved traumas, chronic stress or a feeling of spiritual disconnection. Working with a shaman can help identify these causes and develop strategies to address them. The shaman can use various techniques, including the shamanic journey, where the practitioner enters an altered state of consciousness to connect with their spiritual guides and gain insights into the roots of the addiction.

Shamanic rituals are an essential part of this process. They help restore the individual's energy balance and promote emotional and spiritual healing. For example, a release ritual can be performed to help the person let go of the negative energies and influences associated with the addiction. This ritual can include burning symbols of the addiction or performing a water purification ceremony.

The integration of daily practices, such as meditation, visualization and the use of positive affirmations, is also crucial to support recovery. Meditation can help calm the mind and develop greater self-awareness, while visualization can be used to strengthen the intention to heal and visualize a future free from addiction. Positive affirmations, such as "I am strong and capable of overcoming this addiction", can reinforce confidence and determination.

The road to recovery from addictions is challenging and requires an ongoing commitment to healing and self-knowledge. By integrating shamanic practices and addressing the underlying causes of addictions, it is possible to promote deep and sustainable recovery. The journey is unique to each individual, and the support of spiritual guides and mentors can be invaluable in maintaining progress and motivation along the way.

Healing from addictions through shamanic practices involves various processes and rituals that seek to restore balance and harmony to the individual. One of the most effective methods is the shamanic journey, where the shaman enters an altered state of consciousness to seek guidance from the guiding spirits. During this journey, the shaman can identify the spiritual and emotional causes of the addiction and gain insight into the steps needed for healing.

The shamanic journey is often initiated with the rhythmic sound of drums or rattles, which help to alter the state of consciousness and facilitate entry into the spirit world. The shaman may encounter power animals or spirit guides who offer wisdom and support for healing. These guides can help identify past traumas or energetic imbalances that contribute to addiction, and provide guidance on how to restore harmony.

Another powerful practice is soul retrieval. Many addictions are rooted in deep traumas that fragment the individual's soul, creating a sense of emptiness and disconnection. Soul retrieval involves the shaman traveling to the spirit world to retrieve lost parts of the soul, reintegrating them into the individual and restoring their integrity. This process can be profoundly transformative, helping to heal the emotional wounds that sustain addiction.

In addition to the journey and the recovery of the soul, purification rituals are essential in the treatment of addictions. Purification can involve burning sacred herbs such as sage, which helps to cleanse negative energies from the body and the environment. Herbal baths or smoking can also be used to purify the individual's energy field, removing blockages and promoting the free flow of vital energy.

Liberation rituals are equally important. These rituals help the person to release negative emotions, destructive thought patterns and spiritual influences that contribute to addiction. A release ritual can include writing negative feelings and experiences on a piece of paper and burning this paper, symbolizing the release of these energies. The ceremony can be accompanied by chants and prayers that reinforce the intention of healing and transformation.

Integrating the spiritual experiences and insights gained during the rituals is crucial for long-term recovery. This can be done through daily practices such as meditation, which helps keep the mind calm and focused, and visualization, which reinforces the intentions of healing and positive change. Daily affirmations are also useful for reprogramming the mind with positive and constructive thoughts, replacing negative thought patterns that sustain addiction.

Community support is another vital element in healing from addictions. Participating in healing circles or support groups can provide a sense of belonging and emotional support. Sharing experiences and receiving support from others who are on the same journey can strengthen resolve and offer new perspectives. The feeling of community and connection with others can be a powerful motivator for continuing recovery.

In addition, practicing gratitude can have a significant impact on recovery. Taking a moment every day to reflect on the things you are grateful for can help shift the focus of the mind from problems and addictions to positive aspects of life. This can create a more balanced and positive state of mind, promoting emotional and spiritual well-being.

Healing from addictions through shamanism is a deep and multifaceted process that addresses all dimensions of being - physical, emotional, mental and spiritual. By integrating these practices and rituals, it is possible not only to overcome addiction, but also to profoundly transform one's life, finding a new sense of balance, purpose and spiritual connection. The path is challenging, but with the support of spiritual guides, mentors and a supportive community, recovery is possible and sustainable.

Recovery from addictions is an ongoing process that requires a constant commitment to self-care and reintegration into everyday life. In addition to rituals and spiritual practices, it is essential to adopt self-care strategies that support physical, mental and emotional health. These strategies help build a solid foundation for recovery and prevent relapse.

One of the first self-care strategies is to establish a structured daily routine. Keeping regular schedules for sleeping, eating and activities can help create a sense of stability and predictability, which is crucial for recovery. A structured routine can include moments dedicated to meditation, physical exercise, and recreational activities that promote well-being.

Regular physical exercise is particularly important in addiction recovery. Physical activity not only helps to improve physical health, but also releases endorphins, which are hormones that promote well-being and happiness. Activities such as walking, running, yoga or tai chi can be especially beneficial, as they also help to calm the mind and reduce stress.

Healthy eating is another vital component of self-care. A balanced and nutritious diet can help restore the body and mind by providing the nutrients needed for recovery. Avoiding substances that can trigger addiction, such as alcohol or foods high in sugar and caffeine, is essential. Instead, opting for whole foods, fruits, vegetables, and lean proteins can help maintain energy and focus.

Regular practice of relaxation techniques, such as deep breathing and meditation, is also crucial. Mindful breathing can help calm the nervous system and reduce anxiety, while meditation can promote greater self-awareness and inner peace. Incorporating these practices into the daily routine can help maintain a state of balance and prevent a return to addictive behavior.

Therapy and counseling can be extremely helpful in recovering from addictions. Working with a therapist or counselor can provide emotional support and help address the underlying issues that contributed to the addiction. Therapy can offer practical techniques for dealing with triggers and developing healthy coping skills. In addition, group therapy can provide a sense of community and peer support.

Keeping a recovery journal can be a powerful tool for tracking progress and reflecting on the journey. Writing about daily challenges, successes and insights can help process emotions and reinforce the intention to recover. The journal can also serve as a reminder of goals and reasons to continue on the healing journey.

Connecting with nature is another important element in the recovery process. Spending time outdoors, in parks, forests or near bodies of water, can have a calming and revitalizing effect. Nature offers a tranquil environment that can help restore energy and promote inner reflection. Practicing mindfulness in nature, such as walking barefoot in the grass or meditating outdoors, can strengthen the connection with the natural world and promote healing.

Gratitude rituals also play a significant role in recovery. Taking a moment every day to express gratitude can help refocus the mind on positive aspects of life and cultivate an attitude of appreciation. This can create a more balanced and resilient state of mind, helping to prevent relapse into addictive behavior.

In addition, seeking out new activities and hobbies can be an effective way of filling your time and mind with positive experiences. Finding passions and interests that bring joy and satisfaction can help replace addictive behavior and create a sense of purpose. Whether through art, music, sport or volunteering, these activities can enrich life and offer new ways to find pleasure and fulfillment.

Recovery from addictions is an ongoing process that requires dedication, self-care and a commitment to personal transformation. By integrating self-care practices, seeking support and finding new forms of meaning and joy, it is possible to create a balanced and fulfilling life, free from the bonds of addiction. The journey is challenging, but with the right tools and support, recovery is possible and sustainable.

To ensure that recovery from addictions is sustainable, it is essential to integrate the learnings and practices into everyday life on an ongoing basis. This involves a multi-faceted approach that includes spiritual, emotional and physical support. Sustainability in recovery requires a commitment to personal growth and adapting practices as necessary.

One of the keys to sustainability in recovery is the continuous practice of mindfulness. Mindfulness involves being fully present in the moment, observing thoughts and emotions without judgment. This practice can help identify and manage addiction triggers before they become problematic. Practicing mindfulness daily, even for a few minutes, can strengthen the ability to remain centered and focused.

Connecting with the community is another essential component for sustainability. Participating in support groups and healing circles can offer a sense of belonging and mutual understanding. These groups provide a safe space to share experiences, get feedback and receive encouragement. The feeling of being connected with others facing similar challenges can be a powerful motivating factor.

Rituals and spiritual practices should be maintained and adapted as necessary. Maintaining a personal altar, performing purification rituals and continuing the shamanic journey are all practices that can be adjusted to suit the evolving needs of recovery. These rituals help maintain the connection with the spirit world and reinforce healing intentions.

The practice of gratitude continues to be a powerful tool in maintaining recovery. Gratitude not only helps refocus the mind on positive aspects, but also creates an emotional state that is less susceptible to stress and anxiety. Keeping a gratitude journal, where you regularly record things you are grateful for, can help cultivate a positive and resilient mindset.

Self-reflection is another important practice. Taking time regularly to reflect on progress, challenges and lessons learned can offer valuable insights. Self-reflection can be facilitated through writing in a journal, meditation or conversations with a mentor or therapist. This helps keep recovery in perspective and adjust strategies as necessary.

Developing healthy coping skills is crucial for dealing with the challenges that arise throughout recovery. This can include relaxation techniques such as deep breathing, meditation and physical exercise, as well as practical strategies for managing stress and anxiety. Learning to deal with difficult emotions in a healthy way is an essential skill that supports long-term recovery.

Continuing education about addictions is also important. Reading books, attending lectures and participating in workshops on recovery and wellness can offer new perspectives and reinforce commitment to healing. Continuing education helps you stay informed about best practices and find new tools that can be useful on the recovery journey.

Practicing self-compassion is key. Recognizing that recovery is an ongoing process and treating yourself with kindness during the ups and downs can make a big difference. Self-compassion involves accepting that mistakes and relapses can happen, but that they are opportunities for learning and growth. Treating yourself with love and understanding can strengthen emotional resilience and support ongoing recovery.

Integrating physical wellness practices, such as a balanced diet and regular exercise, is also essential. Keeping the body healthy supports the mind and spirit, creating a solid foundation for recovery. Avoiding substances that can trigger addiction and opting for a nutritious diet helps maintain physical and energetic balance.

Recovery from addictions is an ongoing journey that requires dedication, resilience and support. By integrating spiritual, emotional and physical practices into daily life, it is possible to create a sustainable path of healing and transformation. Through a commitment to self-care, self-reflection and connection with the community, recovery can be sustained and strengthened, leading to a balanced and fulfilling life.

The journey of recovery from addictions is not only about overcoming difficulties, but also about personal and spiritual growth. Building resilience and strengthening the spirit are crucial aspects that help maintain recovery in the long term. This process involves adopting practices and attitudes that promote integral well-being and continuous evolution.

Resilience is the ability to recover quickly from difficulties and adapt to changes and challenges. To build resilience, it is essential to develop a positive and proactive mindset. This can be done by practicing gratitude, maintaining an optimistic outlook and celebrating achievements, no matter how small. Resilience is strengthened when you recognize that challenges are opportunities for learning and growth.

Spiritual growth is a fundamental component of addiction recovery. Connecting with the spiritual world and one's own essence can provide an inexhaustible source of strength and guidance. Spiritual practices such as meditation, prayer, shamanic journeying and nature connection rituals help to deepen this connection. These practices promote introspection, inner peace and a deeper understanding of life's purpose.

One of the most effective ways to promote spiritual growth is through meditation. Regular meditation helps to calm the mind, reduce stress and develop greater self-awareness. There are various forms of meditation that can be explored, from silent meditation to guided meditation and meditation in movement, such as yoga. Finding the form of meditation that resonates best with you is important for maintaining a regular practice.

Rituals to connect with nature are also powerful for spiritual growth. Spending time outdoors, observing the changing seasons, feeling the wind and listening to the sounds of nature, can help restore balance and harmony. These moments of deep connection with nature remind us of the interconnectedness of all things and of our own position in the great fabric of life. Practices such as meditative walking, gardening and contemplating the landscape can be incorporated into the daily routine.

Building a spiritual support network is also essential. Participating in spiritual communities, whether in shamanic support groups or other spiritual traditions, can provide a sense of belonging and ongoing support. These communities offer a safe space to share experiences, learn new practices and receive guidance. The feeling of being connected with others who share similar values and spiritual goals can strengthen determination and motivation on the recovery journey.

The practice of compassion and service to others is also fundamental to spiritual growth. Helping others, whether through voluntary action or simply offering support to friends and family, can bring a deep sense of purpose and fulfillment. Compassion and service help cultivate an altruistic perspective and feel part of something bigger, reinforcing the connection with humanity and the spirit.

Cultivating a mindset of continuous learning is another important aspect of spiritual growth and resilience. Seeking knowledge through reading, attending workshops and studying spiritual practices can enrich the recovery journey. Continuous learning keeps the mind active and engaged, offering new perspectives and tools for dealing with life's challenges.

Finally, practicing self-reflection and self-knowledge is crucial. Taking time to reflect on your own thoughts, emotions and actions helps you develop a deeper understanding of yourself. Self-reflection can be facilitated through writing in a journal, introspective meditation or conversations with a mentor or therapist. This process of self-knowledge is continuous and essential for personal and spiritual growth.

Recovery from addictions is a journey of transformation that involves not only overcoming challenges, but also growing and strengthening the spirit. By adopting practices that promote resilience and spiritual growth, it is possible to maintain recovery and create a full and balanced life. Through connecting with the spiritual world, practicing compassion and service, and committing to continuous learning and self-reflection, recovery can be a journey of discovery and deep personal fulfillment.

Chapter 19
Spiritual Problems

Spiritual problems affect a person's connection with the divine and spirituality itself, and can manifest in a variety of ways. They can appear as a sense of disconnection, loss of faith, or an existential crisis that profoundly impacts emotional and mental well-being.

Identifying the symptoms of spiritual problems is essential to starting the healing process. Common signs include a persistent feeling of emptiness or lack of purpose, difficulty finding joy or meaning in daily activities, and a sense of isolation, even when surrounded by other people. These symptoms can lead to a deterioration in quality of life, affecting both mental and physical health.

The impact of spiritual problems on daily life can be significant. A lack of spiritual connection can result in anxiety, depression, and a general feeling of discontent. People can feel lost, without direction, and unable to find inner peace. This disconnection can lead to self-destructive behavior and a reduced ability to deal with stress and life's challenges.

The causes of spiritual problems are varied and can include emotional trauma, challenging life experiences, and a lack of spiritual support. The loss of a loved one, traumatic experiences, or exposure to negative environments can all contribute to the development of these problems. In addition, the lack of regular spiritual practices or a supportive community can exacerbate the feeling of disconnection.

Addressing these problems requires a holistic approach that considers all aspects of being - physical, emotional, mental and spiritual. Shamanic healing offers various techniques for identifying and treating spiritual problems, including creating a sacred space, performing purification rituals, and connecting with spirit guides.

Creating a sacred space is the first step. This space should be quiet and free of distractions, allowing a deep connection with the spiritual world. Purification of the space can be done by burning sacred herbs, such as sage or cedar, to cleanse negative energies and prepare the environment for healing. Creating a personal altar with elements that symbolize the intention of spiritual healing, such as crystals, candles and spiritual symbols, can help to focus the energy and intention.

Shamanic journeying is a powerful technique for addressing spiritual problems. During the journey, the shaman enters an altered state of consciousness to connect with guide spirits and gain insights into the causes of spiritual problems and appropriate healing methods. The shaman can meet and interact with animal spirits or ancestral guides, who offer wisdom and support. These interactions help to identify the spiritual blockages and imbalances that need to be resolved in order to restore harmony.

Connecting with nature is also fundamental to spiritual healing. Spending time outdoors, meditating in natural places and performing rituals in open environments can help strengthen the connection with the earth and the universe. Nature offers an inexhaustible source of healing energy that can be harnessed to restore spiritual balance. Natural elements such as stones, water, plants and fresh air contribute to the healing process, allowing a reconnection with the natural cycle of life.

Meditation and visualization practices are essential for strengthening the spiritual connection. Guided meditations involving visualizations of light and healing can help transform negative energies and promote a state of inner peace. Visualizing a golden or white light entering the body and filling every cell with healing and love can be a powerful practice for uplifting the spirit and restoring hope.

In addition, participating in healing circles or shamanic support groups can provide a sense of belonging and emotional support. These groups offer a safe space to share experiences and practices, and to receive support from others who are on the same healing journey. The exchange of wisdom and healing techniques can offer new insights and strengthen the determination to move forward. A sense of belonging and connection with others can be a powerful antidote to spiritual problems.

Cultivating self-compassion and acceptance is fundamental to spiritual healing. Recognizing that spiritual problems are a natural part of the human journey and treating yourself with kindness and understanding can lighten the emotional load. Regular practice of self-compassion can help alleviate feelings of guilt or inadequacy and promote a sense of self-acceptance and self-love.

Shamanic healing for spiritual problems involves a holistic approach that considers all aspects of being - physical, emotional, mental and spiritual. By creating an environment conducive to healing, carrying out shamanic journeys, using medicinal plants and incorporating meditation and visualization practices, it is possible to treat spiritual problems in an effective and lasting way. These practices not only help relieve the symptoms of spiritual problems, but also promote holistic health, providing a more balanced and harmonious life.

Shamanic healing rituals play a central role in the treatment of spiritual problems. These rituals are designed to restore harmony between the body, mind and spirit, and to facilitate reconnection with the spiritual world. They can range from simple ceremonies to more elaborate rituals, depending on individual needs.

One of the most common rituals is the purification ceremony. This practice involves cleansing the body and space with the help of sacred herbs such as sage, cedar or palo santo. The smoke from these herbs is used to purify the aura, remove negative energies and prepare the individual for healing.

Purification creates a safe and sacred environment where spiritual healing can take place more effectively.

Shamanic journeying is another essential practice in healing spiritual problems. During the journey, the shaman enters an altered state of consciousness, usually induced by the rhythmic sound of the drum or rattle. This state allows the shaman to travel to the spiritual realms and interact with spirit guides, power animals and ancestors. These entities offer wisdom, guidance and support, helping to identify and treat spiritual blockages.

Soul retrieval is a powerful technique used to treat spiritual and emotional trauma. Often, traumatic events can cause the soul to fragment, resulting in a feeling of emptiness and disconnection. The shaman searches for these lost parts of the soul during the spiritual journey and reintegrates them into the individual. This recovery process helps to restore spiritual integrity and vitality.

The use of medicinal plants is a traditional practice in shamanism, which can be particularly effective in treating spiritual problems. Herbs such as St. John's wort, known for its antidepressant properties, and lavender, which promotes calm, can be integrated into the daily routine. Drinking herbal teas or using essential oils in diffusers can help relieve the symptoms of spiritual problems. In addition, creating a medicinal herb garden can be a therapeutic activity that connects the individual to the earth and promotes well-being.

The practice of meditation and visualization is essential for strengthening the spiritual connection and promoting healing. Guided meditations involving visualizations of light and healing can help transform negative energies and promote a state of inner peace. Visualizing a golden or white light entering the body and filling every cell with healing and love can be a powerful practice for uplifting the spirit and restoring hope. This practice can be done daily upon waking or before going to sleep to reinforce the healing intention.

Conscious breathing exercises are equally important in healing spiritual problems. The regular practice of deep, controlled breathing can help calm the nervous system and reduce the anxiety associated with spiritual problems. Techniques such as diaphragmatic breathing or alternate breathing can be performed several times a day to promote calm and balance. These practices can be incorporated into the daily routine during times of stress or as part of a morning or evening ritual.

Participating in healing circles or shamanic support groups can provide a sense of community and emotional support. These groups offer a safe space to share experiences and practices, and to receive support from others who are on the same healing journey. The exchange of wisdom and healing techniques can offer new insights and strengthen the resolve to move forward. The sense of belonging and connection with others can be a powerful antidote to spiritual problems.

In addition to these practices, it is important to cultivate an attitude of self-compassion and acceptance. Recognizing that spiritual problems are a natural part of the human journey and treating yourself with kindness and understanding can lighten the emotional load. Regular practice of self-compassion can help alleviate feelings of guilt or inadequacy and promote a sense of self-acceptance and self-love.

Shamanic healing for spiritual problems involves a holistic approach that considers all aspects of being - physical, emotional, mental and spiritual. By creating an environment conducive to healing, carrying out shamanic journeys, using medicinal plants and incorporating meditation and visualization practices, it is possible to treat spiritual problems in an effective and lasting way. These practices not only help relieve the symptoms of spiritual problems, but also promote holistic health, providing a more balanced and harmonious life.

The connection with nature is a fundamental element in shamanic healing, especially when it comes to spiritual problems. Nature offers an inexhaustible source of healing energy and an opportunity to reconnect with the natural cycle of life. Spending time outdoors, whether in forests, mountains or near bodies of water, can have a profound impact on spiritual health. The practice of walking barefoot on the earth, also known as grounding, can help realign the body's energy with the energy of the earth, promoting a state of balance and well-being.

Creating personal rituals to connect with nature can be highly beneficial. These rituals can include outdoor meditations, symbolic offerings to the earth, or simply spending time in silence observing the natural beauty around you. These moments of contemplation and connection help to strengthen the relationship with the natural world and find inner peace. In addition, observing natural cycles, such as the phases of the moon and seasonal changes, can help align one's energy with the rhythms of the universe.

Shamanic instruments, such as drums and rattles, are powerful tools for facilitating spiritual healing. The rhythmic sound of the drum can help induce altered states of consciousness, allowing a deeper connection with the spiritual realms. Playing the drum or rattle during meditations or rituals can help focus the mind, release energy blockages and promote healing. Each beat of the drum resonates with the heartbeat of the earth, creating a sense of union and harmony.

The role of the shaman as a facilitator of spiritual healing is crucial. The shaman acts as a guide, helping the individual to navigate the spiritual realms and find the answers and healing needed. During healing sessions, the shaman can use a combination of techniques, including shamanic journeying, soul retrieval and energy purification, to help the individual overcome their spiritual problems. The shaman's ancestral wisdom and connection with the guiding spirits are valuable resources for promoting healing.

The practice of gratitude is another powerful tool in spiritual healing. Expressing gratitude regularly can transform personal energy and promote a sense of contentment and peace. Gratitude helps to focus the mind on the positive aspects of life, reducing the impact of negative energies. Keeping a gratitude journal, where you record three things you are grateful for every day, can be a simple but effective practice to promote spiritual well-being.

Healing crystals are widely used in shamanism to balance and harmonize the body's energy. Each crystal has unique properties that can be used for different healing purposes. Amethyst, for example, is known for its calming properties and spiritual protection, while rose quartz promotes love and inner peace. Placing crystals at strategic points during meditations or rituals, or simply carrying them with you, can amplify healing energy and promote spiritual harmony.

The art of creating a personal altar can be a transformative practice. An altar serves as a focal point for daily spiritual practice, providing a dedicated space for meditation, prayer and reflection. Including elements that symbolize the intention of spiritual healing, such as candles, crystals, plants and sacred symbols, can help focus energy and intention. Keeping the altar clean and organized is essential to ensure that it remains a space for healing and connection.

The practice of self-compassion is vital on the spiritual healing journey. Treating yourself with kindness and understanding, especially during challenging times, can lighten the emotional load and promote a sense of well-being. Self-compassion involves recognizing one's own humanity and imperfection, accepting that everyone faces difficulties and that it is normal to need time and support to heal. Daily self-compassion practices, such as guided meditations focused on self-love or affirming positive thoughts about oneself, can strengthen emotional and spiritual resilience.

Shamanic healing for spiritual problems is an ongoing process that involves the integration of various practices and techniques. By creating an environment conducive to healing, connecting with nature, using shamanic instruments, practicing gratitude, and incorporating healing crystals, it is possible to restore spiritual balance and promote general well-being. These practices, combined with the support of an experienced shaman and the practice of self-compassion, can help overcome spiritual problems and live a fuller, more harmonious life.

Participation in community rituals is a fundamental practice for spiritual healing in shamanism. These rituals strengthen the sense of belonging and community, offering emotional and spiritual support. Taking part in ceremonies such as sacred dances, drum circles and fire rituals can help release negative energies, increase spiritual connection and promote collective healing. The energy shared at these events amplifies healing power and creates a safe space for spiritual transformation.

Integrating spiritual practices into the daily routine is crucial to maintaining balance and harmony. Establishing a daily time for meditation, prayer or reflection can help maintain the connection with the divine and strengthen spirituality. These practices should be seen as sacred moments of self-care, where you can focus on breathing, gratitude and the intention to heal. Constancy in these daily practices reinforces the spiritual connection and promotes a continuous state of well-being.

Dreams are a powerful gateway to spiritual communication and can offer valuable insights into a person's spiritual condition. Keeping a dream journal and writing down dream experiences can help identify patterns and messages from spirit guides. The shaman can help interpret these dreams, offering guidance on how to apply the insights received in everyday life. Dreams often contain symbols and messages which, when understood, can guide the process of healing and self-knowledge.

Practicing moon rituals is another effective way to strengthen spirituality and promote healing. The moon has a profound impact on spiritual energies, and performing rituals during moon phases, such as the full moon and the new moon, can help align healing intentions with natural cycles. During the full moon, release rituals can be performed to let go of negative energies and habits, while the new moon is a powerful time to set new intentions and begin new healing cycles.

The use of mandalas and sacred symbols can be a powerful tool for meditation and spiritual healing. Mandalas are geometric representations of the universe and can be used to focus the mind and promote deep meditation. Drawing or painting mandalas can be a meditative practice in itself, helping to clear the mind and establish a connection with the inner self and the divine. Other sacred symbols, such as the circle, the cross and the spiral, can be incorporated into rituals and meditation practices to amplify the healing intention.

The elements of nature - earth, water, fire and air - play a central role in shamanic healing practices. Each element has unique healing properties and can be invoked during rituals to balance and harmonize the body's energy. Earth represents stability and nourishment, water is linked to emotions and purification, fire symbolizes transformation and renewal, and air is associated with communication and thought. Integrating these elements into rituals and meditations can help restore spiritual balance and promote healing.

The practice of fasting and physical purification is a traditional technique used to cleanse the body and prepare the spirit for healing. Fasting, when done safely and consciously, can help release physical and energetic toxins, creating a state of clarity and receptivity. During fasting, meditation and prayer practices can be intensified to strengthen the spiritual connection. Physical purification through herbal baths or saunas can also help cleanse the body's energy and promote a state of well-being.

The role of spirit guides and power animals is fundamental in shamanic healing. These beings offer protection, wisdom and support during the healing process. Connecting regularly with these guides through meditation, prayer and shamanic journeys can provide a sense of security and ongoing guidance. Identifying and working with one's personal power animal can help to access inner qualities and strengths that are necessary for healing and spiritual growth.

The practice of protective visualizations can be useful for creating a safe environment and protecting you from negative energies. Visualizing a protective light around the body and the space where you live can create a barrier against negative influences. This practice can be integrated into the daily routine, especially before bedtime, to ensure a peaceful sleep and a continuous feeling of protection and security.

Shamanic healing for spiritual problems is a deep and continuous process that requires dedication and a holistic approach. Integrating daily practices, participating in community rituals, working with spirit guides and using the elements of nature are essential steps to restoring spiritual balance. With patience and commitment, it is possible to overcome spiritual problems and live a full and harmonious life, in deep connection with the divine and with one's self.

Integrating healing practices into everyday life is essential for maintaining harmony and spiritual well-being. Shamanic healing is not just a series of rituals or isolated sessions, but a continuous journey of self-discovery and growth. Incorporating these practices into the daily routine helps to sustain the benefits of healing and prevent new spiritual problems from arising.

One of the most effective ways to integrate spiritual healing into daily life is through the practice of gratitude. Taking a moment every morning or evening to reflect on the things you are grateful for can transform personal energy and promote a state of contentment and peace. This simple practice helps to refocus the mind on positive aspects of life, reducing the impact of negative energies.

Keeping a spiritual journal can also be a powerful tool for monitoring progress and reflecting on the healing journey. Writing down thoughts, feelings, dreams and spiritual experiences helps to create a clear vision of one's own growth and the areas that still need attention. This journal can include reflections on meditations, shamanic journeys and rituals, as well as insights and messages received from spiritual guides.

Conscious breathing practices are vital for maintaining emotional and spiritual balance. Deep, controlled breathing techniques, such as diaphragmatic breathing, can be performed several times a day to promote calm and relaxation. Conscious breathing helps to calm the nervous system and reduce stress, creating a state of inner peace that is essential for spiritual health.

Participating in creative activities can also be an effective way of integrating spiritual healing into daily life. Activities such as painting, sculpture, dance and music allow for emotional and spiritual expression in a way that words often cannot. Art as a spiritual practice is not about creating something perfect, but about allowing energy to flow freely and connecting with the inner self. This creative expression can be a powerful form of healing and self-discovery.

Practicing simple, daily rituals can help maintain the connection with the divine and reinforce the healing intention. Lighting a candle, burning incense, or performing a short morning meditation are examples of rituals that can be easily incorporated into the daily routine. These small acts of devotion help to establish a sacred space and start the day with a sense of purpose and spiritual alignment.

Regularly connecting with nature is fundamental to maintaining spiritual health. Spending time outdoors, even just for a few minutes every day, can have a profound impact on well-being. Nature offers a source of healing and revitalizing energy, and regular interaction with it helps maintain energy balance. Walking barefoot on the earth, meditating beside a river, or simply watching the stars are all practices that help strengthen the connection with the natural world and restore spiritual balance.

Building a supportive community is crucial for ongoing healing. Participating in healing circles, meditation groups or other spiritual communities offers a safe space to share experiences and receive support. The feeling of belonging and being understood by others who are on the same journey can provide a solid foundation for healing. The exchange of wisdom and healing techniques within this community can enrich one's own spiritual practice and provide new insights and inspiration.

Developing a trusting relationship with a mentor or spiritual guide can be extremely beneficial. Having someone experienced and wise to offer guidance and support can help navigate spiritual challenges and maintain focus on the healing journey. This mentor can be a shaman, a spiritual therapist, or a respected member of the spiritual community. The ongoing wisdom and support of a mentor can be invaluable for spiritual growth.

The practice of self-acceptance and self-compassion is fundamental to spiritual healing. Recognizing and accepting one's own imperfections and challenges as part of the human journey is essential for growth and healing. Treating oneself with kindness and understanding, especially during difficult times, helps to lighten the emotional load and promote a state of well-being. Self-compassion involves recognizing one's own humanity and imperfection, accepting that everyone faces difficulties and that it is normal to need time and support to heal.

Shamanic healing for spiritual problems is an ongoing journey of self-discovery and growth. Integrating daily practices, maintaining a connection with nature, participating in spiritual communities and cultivating self-compassion are essential steps to maintaining harmony and spiritual well-being. With dedication and commitment, it is possible to overcome spiritual problems and live a full and harmonious life, in deep connection with the divine and with one's own self.

Chapter 20
Energy Problems

Energy problems are issues that affect an individual's vitality and general balance, interfering with their ability to function optimally. These problems can manifest in a variety of ways, including feelings of constant tiredness, lack of motivation, difficulty concentrating, among other symptoms. Early and accurate identification of energetic problems is crucial to starting an effective and lasting healing process.

The first step in addressing energy problems is to understand the common symptoms. Feeling constantly tired, even after a good night's sleep, is one of the most obvious signs of an energetic imbalance. In addition, difficulty maintaining concentration or feeling "disconnected" are indications that vital energy may be blocked or unbalanced.

Another common manifestation of energy problems is irritability with no apparent cause. People suffering from energetic imbalances often find themselves reacting disproportionately to everyday situations, which can negatively affect their relationships and work environment. In addition, physical problems such as frequent headaches, digestive problems and muscle pain can be symptoms that something is not right with the body's energy flow.

Identifying these issues involves an introspective process where the individual needs to pay attention to their sensations and emotional states. Keeping a symptom diary can be a useful tool for recognizing patterns and identifying specific times when symptoms are most intense. This can provide valuable insights into possible triggers or underlying causes of energy problems.

A holistic approach to identifying energetic problems also considers external factors that may be contributing to the imbalance. Stressful work environments, toxic relationships or unhealthy lifestyle habits are often correlated with energetic problems. Assessing and, if possible, modifying these factors can be an important initial step in restoring energetic balance.

Practicing self-care techniques is essential for maintaining energetic balance. Incorporating daily activities that promote relaxation and regeneration, such as meditation, practicing yoga, or walking in nature, can help restore the body's natural energy flow. These practices not only relieve immediate stress, but also strengthen long-term emotional and physical resilience.

With the clear identification of energetic problems and a holistic approach to tackling them, it is possible to start on a path of healing and restoring vitality. Integrating daily vital energy care practices can significantly transform quality of life, promoting a state of physical, emotional and spiritual well-being.

After identifying the symptoms and contributing factors to energetic problems, the next step is accurate diagnosis. Diagnosis in the context of shamanic healing involves both self-observation and consultation with experienced practitioners who can offer a deeper insight into energetic issues.

A common tool used in energy diagnosis is aura reading. The aura is an energy field that surrounds the body and can reveal a lot about a person's state of health. Experienced aura reading practitioners can identify areas of energy imbalance or blockage. This practice involves observing the colors, patterns and flows in the aura to detect anomalies that may be contributing to energetic problems.

Another effective diagnostic technique is the use of healing crystals. Certain crystals are known for their energy amplifying and harmonizing properties. Placing specific crystals on different parts of the body can help identify areas of blockage or imbalance. For example, amethyst is often used to diagnose problems related to stress and anxiety, while clear quartz can be used to reveal general imbalances in the energy field.

Guided meditation is another valuable practice for diagnosing energy problems. During meditation, the practitioner can be guided to visualize their own energetic body, identifying areas that seem dark, opaque or blocked. This visualization can be an indication of where the energetic problems are located and can guide the subsequent healing process.

Consulting an experienced shaman or healer is also a crucial step in diagnosing energetic problems. These practitioners have the ability to enter altered states of consciousness and connect with spirit guides who can offer insights into the cause of imbalances. Through healing ceremonies and shamanic journeys, they can identify not only the symptoms, but also the underlying causes of energetic problems.

In addition to specific techniques, observation of the individual's habits and lifestyle is essential for a complete diagnosis. Eating habits, levels of physical activity, sleep patterns and the quality of interpersonal relationships are all factors that influence the energetic state. A detailed diary of these activities can help both the individual and the practitioner to identify patterns that contribute to energetic problems.

Once the diagnosis has been made, it is important to discuss and understand the possible causes of the imbalances. These causes can be multiple and interconnected, including physical, emotional, mental and spiritual factors. Recognizing this interconnectedness is fundamental to addressing energetic problems holistically and effectively.

The energy scan technique can also be used for diagnosis. This involves running your hands over the body, without touching it, to feel variations in the temperature and density of the energy field. Areas that feel cold or dense may indicate blockages or imbalances that need to be treated. This technique can be carried out by the individual themselves or by an experienced healer.

By combining these various diagnostic techniques, it is possible to obtain a comprehensive and detailed view of energetic problems. With an accurate diagnosis, the path to healing becomes clearer, allowing the implementation of specific and effective healing practices. Continued observation and adjustment of practices ensures that the energetic balance is maintained, promoting integral and lasting health.

After an accurate diagnosis of the energetic problems, the next step is to implement healing techniques that promote balance and harmony in the body and spirit. Shamanic healing practices are varied and aim to treat the individual holistically, addressing physical, emotional, mental and spiritual aspects.

A fundamental healing technique is the use of crystals. Crystals such as quartz, amethyst, citrine and black tourmaline are known for their healing properties and energetic balance. Placing crystals at specific points on the body or around the environment can help restore the flow of energy. For example, black tourmaline can be used for protection and the removal of negative energies, while quartz can amplify healing intentions.

Another effective practice is sound therapy, which uses vibrational frequencies to adjust and harmonize the body's energy. Instruments such as drums, Tibetan bowls and bells are often used in shamanic ceremonies. The rhythmic, repetitive sound helps induce deep meditative states, allowing blocked energy to move and rebalance. In addition, chants and mantras can be sung to raise the energetic vibration and promote healing.

The shamanic journey is one of the most powerful techniques in the shaman's arsenal. During a journey, the shaman enters an altered state of consciousness, usually induced by the rhythmic sound of the drum, in order to travel to the spirit world. There, they seek guidance and healing from spirit guides, power animals and ancestors. These journeys can reveal the root causes of energetic problems and provide specific, personalized solutions for the individual.

The practice of purification rituals is also essential in healing energetic problems. Smoking with sacred herbs, such as sage, cedar or palo santo, helps to cleanse negative energies from the body and the environment. The smoke from these herbs has purifying properties and can be used before healing ceremonies or daily as an energy maintenance practice. Smoking should be done with clear intention and focus, moving the smoke around the body and through the living spaces.

Guided meditation is a technique that can be used daily to maintain energetic balance. Meditations focused on visualizing healing lights, such as a white or golden light, flowing through the body, can help dissolve blockages and restore vitality. Visualizing yourself in a safe and sacred place, such as a forest or a field of flowers, can provide a sense of peace and rejuvenation.

The use of medicinal plants is a traditional practice in shamanism that can support energy healing. Herbal infusions such as chamomile, lemon balm and lavender can help relax the body and mind, promoting a state conducive to healing. In addition to teas, essential oils from these plants can be used in diffusers or applied directly to the body for therapeutic benefits. Plants are seen as spiritual allies, and their use should be done with respect and intention.

The practice of grounding is crucial to maintaining energetic balance. Walking barefoot on the earth, gardening or simply sitting in nature can help release excessive energy and absorb the stabilizing energy of the earth. Grounding helps to anchor the body's energy, promoting a state of calm and balance.

Participating in healing circles and spiritual communities can also be very beneficial. These groups offer emotional and spiritual support, allowing individuals to share their experiences and learn new healing practices. The sense of community and belonging can strengthen the healing process and provide new perspectives and insights.

By integrating these healing techniques into everyday life, it is possible to effectively treat energetic problems and promote a state of balance and harmony. Shamanic healing, with its holistic and profound approach, offers a powerful path to integral health and well-being, providing a life that is fuller and more connected to the universe.

Once energy balance has been achieved, it is essential to implement maintenance practices to ensure that harmony is preserved. Regular maintenance of energetic balance is vital for preventing problems from returning and for sustaining integral health in the long term.

A fundamental practice for maintaining energetic balance is daily meditation. Setting aside a specific time each day to meditate can help clear the mind of negative thoughts and keep energy flowing smoothly through the body. Guided meditations that focus on visualizing healing lights or connecting with nature can be particularly beneficial. This daily practice not only helps maintain balance, but also promotes a continuous state of peace and well-being.

The regular practice of grounding remains crucial. Activities such as walking barefoot in the grass, sitting on the earth or hugging a tree help to connect with the stabilizing energy of the earth. These moments of connection with nature are powerful for anchoring the body's energy and releasing any built-up tension. Incorporating these activities into your daily or weekly routine can make a significant difference to your energy balance.

The use of healing crystals as part of energy maintenance is highly recommended. Keeping crystals such as amethyst, rose quartz and black tourmaline around the living space or in the work environment can help maintain a clean and balanced energy field. In addition, carrying small crystals in your pocket or wearing them as jewelry can provide continuous protection and energetic balance throughout the day.

Practicing regular purification rituals, such as smoking, is essential for keeping the environment energetically clean. Burning sacred herbs such as sage, cedar or palo santo once a week, or as needed, helps to remove accumulated negative energies and renew the space with positive energy. These rituals should be carried out with a clear intention and a conscious focus on cleansing and protecting the space.

Keeping a gratitude journal is a simple but effective technique for maintaining energy balance. Writing daily about the things you are grateful for helps raise your emotional and mental vibration, promoting a continuous state of contentment and peace.

Practicing gratitude transforms negative energy into positive energy and creates an internal environment conducive to well-being.

Participating in healing circles and spiritual communities on a regular basis is another way to maintain energy balance. These gatherings provide ongoing support, an exchange of knowledge and the opportunity to take part in group healing ceremonies. Connecting with others who share similar practices strengthens the determination and motivation to maintain self-care practices.

Physical self-care is equally important. Maintaining a routine of regular exercise, healthy eating and adequate sleep contributes significantly to maintaining energy balance. Physical activities such as yoga, tai chi or walking help to release tension and promote a healthy energy flow. Eating a nutrient-rich diet, avoiding processed foods and stimulants such as caffeine and sugar, is also crucial to sustaining vital energy.

Using essential oils as part of your daily routine can provide ongoing benefits for energy balance. Oils such as lavender, chamomile and eucalyptus can be used in diffusers, added to baths or applied directly to the skin to promote relaxation and energetic cleansing. These oils have therapeutic properties that help maintain a state of calm and well-being.

The practice of conscious breathing is a technique that can be incorporated at any time of the day. Simple breathing exercises, such as diaphragmatic breathing or the 4-7-8 technique, help to calm the nervous system and keep the mind and body balanced. Taking regular breaks throughout the day to practice conscious breathing can prevent the build-up of stress and tension.

Maintaining energy balance is an ongoing commitment that requires dedication and regular practice. By integrating these techniques and practices into daily life, it is possible to sustain a state of harmony and vitality, promoting integral health and a deep connection with the universe. Maintaining energy balance not only prevents future problems, but also enriches life, providing a fuller and more conscious experience.

As well as maintaining energetic balance, it is essential to strengthen and protect the body's energy to ensure lasting health and resilience against negative influences. Various shamanic practices and holistic techniques can be implemented for this purpose.

One of the first steps to strengthening energy is to work with the chakras, the body's energy centers. Each chakra is associated with specific aspects of physical, emotional and spiritual health. Practicing meditations focused on each chakra can help balance and strengthen these centers. Visualizing specific colors, such as red for the root chakra or blue for the throat chakra, while concentrating on each area, can help activate and harmonize energy.

Conscious eating also plays a crucial role in strengthening energy. Consuming foods rich in prana, or vital energy, such as fresh fruit, vegetables, nuts and seeds, can increase the body's vitality. Avoiding processed foods, refined sugars and stimulants such as caffeine helps to keep energy clean and balanced. Adequate hydration is also vital; drinking pure, fresh water throughout the day helps maintain the flow of vital energy.

Regular practice of physical activities that promote the flow of energy is essential. Yoga, tai chi and qi gong are particularly effective for moving and strengthening the body's energy. These practices combine movement, breathing and meditation, helping to release energy blockages and increase physical and emotional resilience.

Strengthening energy also involves constantly connecting with nature. Spending time outdoors, absorbing the revitalizing energy of the earth, air, water and sun, is fundamental. Practices such as hugging trees, swimming in natural waters or simply walking barefoot in the grass can recharge vital energy and strengthen the connection with the natural world.

Protecting energy is another vital aspect to ensure that the balance achieved is maintained. An effective technique is to visualize protective shields. Before starting the day, taking a few minutes to visualize a protective light around the body can create a barrier against negative influences. This light can be any color that resonates with the feeling of protection, such as white, gold or blue. Reinforcing this visualization with the repetition of protective mantras, such as "I am protected and safe", strengthens the intention and effectiveness of the shield.

The use of amulets and talismans can also provide energetic protection. Stones such as black tourmaline, obsidian and tiger's eye are known for their protective properties. Carrying these stones in your pocket or wearing them as jewelry can help repel negative energies and keep your aura clean. In addition, creating personalized amulets, imbued with specific intentions, can provide an extra layer of protection.

Participating in shamanic protection ceremonies on a regular basis is another powerful way to keep your energy safe. These ceremonies can include invoking guardian spirits, creating protection circles and performing purification rituals. The shaman can guide the participant in creating a sacred and safe space where negative energy cannot penetrate.

The practice of energy cleansing rituals in the living and working environment is equally important. Regularly smoking these spaces with sacred herbs, such as sage or palo santo, helps to remove any accumulated negative energy and create a protected and harmonious environment. Keeping the space clean and organized also contributes to the free flow of positive energy.

Maintaining healthy relationships is crucial for energy protection. Toxic relationships can drain energy and create imbalances. Setting clear boundaries and practicing open and honest communication helps protect one's energy. Surrounding yourself with supportive and uplifting people is essential for maintaining a positive energetic state.

Finally, the regular practice of self-compassion and self-care is vital for strengthening and protecting energy. Treating yourself with kindness, recognizing your own needs and dedicating time to daily self-care promotes long-lasting energetic resilience. Activities such as herbal baths, massages and moments of relaxation are essential for recharging and protecting energy.

By integrating these energy-boosting and energy-protecting practices into your daily routine, you can create a solid foundation for integral health and ongoing resilience against negative influences. These practices not only help maintain energy balance, but also promote a life full of vitality, spiritual connection and well-being.

Epilogue

As I come to the end of this journey through the practices and wisdom of shamanism, I want to express my deepest gratitude to you. The decision to embark on this journey of healing and self-knowledge is a courageous and transformative step, and I sincerely hope that the techniques and teachings presented in this book have provided you with valuable insights and a clear path to achieving balance and harmony in your life.

The practice of shamanism teaches us that we are all interconnected, not just with each other, but with the universe and with nature. It is this interconnection that allows us to access true and deep healing, and it is my hope that you have found in this book the tools you need to strengthen this connection in your own life.

As well as thanking you, the reader, I would like to express my deepest gratitude to the incredible research and support team that made this book possible. To the dedicated researchers who delved into the ancient traditions and contemporary practices of shamanism, your contributions were invaluable. Your dedication to seeking out and validating information, often facing challenges and overcoming obstacles, has been essential in ensuring that this book is a reliable and enriching source of knowledge.

To the editorial team, whose keen eye and refined skill transformed raw manuscripts into a cohesive and accessible text, your tireless work and attention to detail ensured that every word resonates with clarity and purpose. His passion for this project was palpable at every stage of the process, and I am eternally grateful for his collaboration.

Finally, I thank my friends and family for their continued support and encouragement. Their patience and understanding were fundamental in allowing me to devote the time and energy needed to create this work.

May this book be a light on your journey, guiding you towards a life of balance, healing and spiritual connection. May the teachings and practices shared here flourish in your life, bringing peace, harmony and a deeper understanding of yourself and the world around you.

With gratitude and respect,

Luan Ferr

Bibliographic References

"El Manuscrito Sagrado de los Andes" - Ancestral Treatise of Andean Shamanism. Q'ero Inka, Ed. 1210.

"Тайны Сибирского Шаманизма" (Secrets of Siberian Shamanism) - Treatise of Tundra Healers. Evenki Village, Ed. 1100.

"The Path of the Apache Healer" - Spiritual Traditions of the Apaches. Born Laughing, Ed. 1340.

"O Livro das Ervas de Cura Amazônicas" - Knowledge of Yanomami Shamanism. Eldar Yanomami, Ed. 1230.

"الـ بربـر شـيوخ معرفة" (The Wisdom of the Desert) - Shamanic Practices of the Berbers. Ait El Caid, Ed. 1150.

"Te Mātauranga o ngā Tīpuna Māori" - Healing Rituals of Aotearoa. Te Kooti Arikirangi, Ed. 1300.

"Healing Arts of the San People" - Ancestral Medicine of the Kalahari Desert. Kagiso, Ed. 1250.

"Il Manoscritto del Guaritore Sardo" - Shamanic Traditions of Sardinia. Antonia Pisanu, Ed. 1190.

"Le Manuscrit des Sages Celtes" - Healing Rituals of the Druids. Cernunnos MacRoich, Ed. 1050.

"Abenaki Healing Practices" - Ancestral Knowledge of the Abenaki. Kchi Wados, Ed. 1280.

"तांत्रिक चिकित्सा का रहस्य" (The Secret of Tantric Medicine) - Shamanic Practices of India. Acharya Shankara, Ed. 1400.

"秘教の知恵" (Wisdom of Esotericism) - Treatise of Japanese Shamanic Healing. Yamabushi Satoru, Ed. 1370.

"Arte Curativa dos Tupinambás" - Shamanic Knowledge of Brazil. Pindarô Mirim, Ed. 1260.

"秘伝の医術" (Secret Art of Medicine) - Healing Rituals of Japan. Hikari Mori, Ed. 1320.

"Şifa Sanatları" - Shamanic Practices of Anatolia. Derviş Mehmet, Ed. 1450.

"Las Artes Curativas de los Mapuches" - Ancestral Medicine of Chile. Lonko Antumapu, Ed. 1220.

"De helande konster av samerna" - Shamanic Knowledge of Lapland. Niillas Ailu, Ed. 1180.

"El Libro de los Conjuros de los Mayas" - Maya Healing Rituals. Itzamnaaj Balam, Ed. 1350.

"Le Savoir des Anciens Gaulois" - Shamanic Healing Practices of the Gauls. Ambrosius Aurelianus, Ed. 1230.

"Shamanic Healing Practices of the Ojibwa" - Ancestral Knowledge of the Ojibwa. Migizi, Ed. 1290.

"Artes de Cura dos Guarani" - Shamanic Medicine of Paraguay. Karai Pora, Ed. 1210.

"Oshe Nipa Egungun" - Shamanic Practices of the Yoruba. Babalaô Femi, Ed. 1280.

"Традиционные знания шаманов бурят" (Traditional Knowledge of the Buryat Shamans) - Ancestral Medicine of Siberia. Bayan Khaan, Ed. 1140.

"Healers of the Hawaiian Islands" - Shamanic Knowledge of Hawaii. Kahuna Lani, Ed. 1250.

"Antigos Rituais de Cura dos Celtas" - Shamanic Practices of Ireland. Eithne Ní Bhraonáin, Ed. 1100.

www.ingramcontent.com/pod-product-compliance
Lightning Source LLC
LaVergne TN
LVHW040047080526
838202LV00045B/3525